Original Title: Discovering Spain.

© Discovering Spain, Carlos Martínez Cerdá and Víctor Martínez Cerdá, 2024.

Authors: Víctor Martínez Cerdá and Carlos Martínez Cerdá (V&C Brothers).

© Cover and illustrations: V&C Brothers.

Layout and design: V&C Brothers.

All rights reserved.

This publication may not be wholly or partially reproduced, stored, recorded, or transmitted in any form or by any means, whether mechanical, photochemical, electronic, magnetic, electro-optical, photocopying, or through information retrieval systems, or any other present or future method, without the prior written permission of the copyright holders.

DISCOVERING SPAIN

101 SURPRISING CURIOSITIES

1

In Spain, several languages are spoken due to its rich cultural and linguistic diversity.

Spanish or Castilian is the official language of Spain across the entire country and is spoken by approximately 99% of the population.

Its origin dates back to the Vulgar Latin that evolved in the Iberian Peninsula after the fall of the Roman Empire.

Catalan is a co-official language in Catalonia, the Balearic Islands, and the Valencian Community, where it is called Valencian.

It is spoken by around 9 million people, primarily in Catalonia.

Its origin also comes from Vulgar Latin and developed from the Romance languages spoken in the northeast of the peninsula.

Galician is a co-official language in Galicia and is spoken by approximately 2.4 million people.

Like Spanish and Catalan, it comes from Vulgar Latin, and its evolution is closely related to Portuguese, as both languages share a common root before diverging into different languages.

Basque or Euskera is a co-official language in the Basque Country and parts of Navarre, with approximately 750,000 speakers.

Unlike the other languages, its origin is very ancient and is not related to Latin or any other known language, which makes it a unique language.

Aranese is a dialect of Occitan that is co-official in the Aran Valley in Catalonia and has fewer than 5,000 speakers.

It's a Romance language that developed from Vulgar Latin and is a variety of Gascon, a dialect of Occitan.

Aragonese doesn't have official status, but it is recognized as a native language in Aragon and has about 25,000 speakers.

It is a Romance language that, like Spanish, originated from Vulgar Latin.

Astur-Leonese, also known as Asturian or Bable and Leonese, is recognized as a native language in Asturias and Castile and León, but it doesn't have official status.

Around 150,000 people speak it, and, like the other Romance languages, it also originated from Vulgar Latin.

In addition to these, there are other languages and dialects on the peninsula, although with fewer speakers and less official recognition.

Regional languages in Spain reflect the country's cultural and historical diversity, and linguistic policies vary by region to encourage their use and preservation.

2

The Camino de Santiago is a historic pilgrimage route that leads to the Cathedral of Santiago de Compostela, where the remains of the Apostle James the Greater are said to rest.

-Origins: The tradition of the Camino dates back to the early 9th century when, according to legend, the remains of the Apostle James were discovered in Galicia. This marked the beginning of the veneration of the Apostle and the pilgrimage to his tomb.

-Routes: There are multiple routes leading to Santiago de Compostela, the most well-known being the French Way, the Northern Way, the Portuguese Way, and the Original Way. Each offers different landscapes and challenges.

-World Heritage: The French Way and the Northern Way are recognized as UNESCO World Heritage Sites due to their historical and cultural significance.

-Pilgrim's Credential: Pilgrims on the Camino carry a "credential" that gives them access to special accommodations called albergues. Upon arrival in Santiago, they can obtain the Compostela, a certificate that attests to their pilgrimage.

-Symbolism: The symbol of the Camino is the scallop shell, which pilgrims historically collected upon reaching Santiago as proof of their journey. Today, it is used to mark the routes.

-Motivations: Although it was originally an act of religious devotion, today many pilgrims walk the Camino for personal, spiritual, sporting, or simply cultural experiences.

-Feast of the Apostle James: July 25 is St. James Day, when thousands of pilgrims gather in Santiago de Compostela to celebrate this festival, which has special significance when it falls in a Jacobean Holy Year.

3

La Sagrada Familia, formally known as the Basilica and Expiatory Church of the Holy Family, is one of the most iconic structures in Barcelona and one of the most renowned architectural works in the world.

1. History: The construction of the Sagrada Familia began in 1882, initially under the direction of architect Francisco de Paula del Villar. A year later, Antoni Gaudí took over the project and radically transformed its design.

2. Gaudí: Antoni Gaudí dedicated much of his life to this project, from 1883 until his death in 1926. He significantly altered the original design, incorporating his characteristic modernist style.

3. Architectural Features:

-Facades: The church has three main facades: the Nativity Facade, the Passion Facade, and the Glory Facade. Each represents different stages in the life of Jesus.

-Towers: The final design includes 18 towers: 12 dedicated to the apostles, 4 to the evangelists, one to Jesus, and one to Mary. The interior has columns that resemble trees, creating the sensation of a forest.

-Symbolism: Every element of the Sagrada Familia has symbolic meaning, whether religious or natural. Gaudí was a devout Catholic, and his faith deeply influenced the design.

-Ongoing Construction: Construction has been ongoing for over a century. After Gaudí's death, work slowed down due to a lack of funds and the Spanish Civil War. Construction resumed at the end of the 20th century.

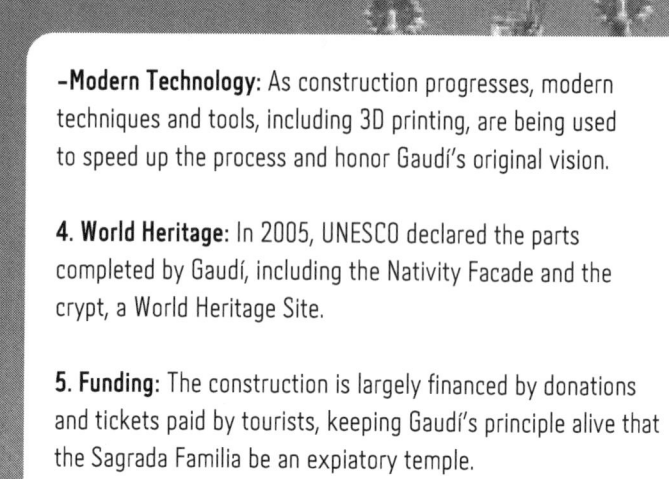

-Modern Technology: As construction progresses, modern techniques and tools, including 3D printing, are being used to speed up the process and honor Gaudí's original vision.

4. World Heritage: In 2005, UNESCO declared the parts completed by Gaudí, including the Nativity Facade and the crypt, a World Heritage Site.

5. Funding: The construction is largely financed by donations and tickets paid by tourists, keeping Gaudí's principle alive that the Sagrada Familia be an expiatory temple.

6. Completion Date: The temple is expected to be completed by 2026, coinciding with the centenary of Gaudí's death.

4

Ham is a fundamental part of Spanish gastronomic culture, being one of the most appreciated and well-known products both in the country and abroad.

The tradition of ham dates back to Roman times, but it was during the Middle Ages that the technique of curing and preserving meat was consolidated.

Ham is a symbol of Spanish gastronomy and is commonly found at celebrations and events.

Slicing ham is an art, and professional slicers are highly valued for their skill.

It is usually eaten alone, in tapas, or as an ingredient in multiple dishes.

The "ham sandwich" is a classic.

Regarding types of ham, Iberian Ham comes from the Iberian pig, a native breed that is mainly raised in the southwestern regions of Spain.

It is classified based on the pigs' diet: Bellota Iberian Ham comes from pigs fed exclusively on acorns during the "montanera," the final fattening stage.

Cebo de Campo Iberian Ham comes from pigs fed on natural feed and pasture in the field, while Cebo Iberian Ham comes from pigs fed on feed in farms.

The recognized denominations of origin for Iberian ham are Guijuelo Ham, Huelva Ham, Los Pedroches Ham, and Dehesa de Extremadura Ham.

Serrano Ham, on the other hand, comes from the white pig, a breed different from the Iberian pig.

It is classified into three categories: Bodega, which is cured between 9 and 12 months; Reserva, cured between 12 and 15 months; and Gran Reserva, which is cured for more than 15 months.

Serrano hams are produced throughout Spain, but the Protected Designation of Origin "Teruel Ham" is one of the best known.

The curing process involves salting and drying, which gives the ham its characteristic texture and flavor.

The curing time varies among the types of ham.

Ham slicing is crucial to maximize its flavor, and it is traditionally done by hand. The ideal slice is thin and elongated.

Iberian ham is considered one of the most expensive products in the world, with some pieces auctioned for thousands of euros.

There are ham museums in different parts of Spain, dedicated to the history and culture of ham.

5

**La Tomatina is a famous festival held in Buñol,
a small town in the Valencian Community.**

This annual event takes place on the last Wednesday of August and is known worldwide as a tomato fight, where participants throw tomatoes at each other for fun.

-History: The first Tomatina was held in 1945. Although the exact origin of the festival is uncertain, it is said to have begun when a group of young people started a fight by throwing tomatoes at each other during a parade. In the 1950s, the event was banned, but it was legalized in 1957 after a symbolic protest in which the locals carried a coffin with a large tomato. Since then, the festival has been held regularly, except for some years due to exceptional circumstances.

-Event Development: The tomatoes used are usually grown for this specific purpose and are not suitable for consumption. They generally come from the Extremadura region.
To maintain safety, there are basic rules such as crushing the tomatoes before throwing them to prevent injuries and not throwing hard objects. The event is extremely popular, and now requires attendees to purchase tickets to limit the number of participants to around 20,000, as it attracts tourists from all over the world.

-Impact: La Tomatina has become a major tourist attraction, contributing significantly to the local economy.
In addition to the main battle, the week leading up to the event includes other festivals, concerts, and cultural events, enriching the visitor experience. La Tomatina is a unique manifestation of joy, where people come together to enjoy a singular experience.

6

Spain is home to a remarkable number of millenary olive trees, considered true natural monuments.

These trees, over a thousand years old, are mainly found in the northeastern regions of the country, especially in the Valencian Community, Catalonia, and Aragon.

-Characteristics: Some of these olive trees have surpassed the millennium mark, making them some of the longest-lived trees on the planet. These olive trees generally have enormous, twisted trunks, giving them a distinctive and majestic appearance. Some specimens have circumferences of several meters. Although many of these trees still produce olives, their yield is usually lower compared to younger olive trees.

-Importance: They symbolize ancient agriculture and olive cultivation in the Mediterranean region. They provide shelter for a wide variety of fauna and flora, playing an important role in the ecosystem. They are part of the identity of the regions where they are found and have been a constant element in the lives of local communities.

-Protection and Tourism: Given their importance, there are efforts to preserve these olive trees, including legislative measures that protect them from being cut down or relocated. The millenary olive trees have become a tourist attraction, and there are routes and guided tours available for those who want to appreciate their beauty and learn about their history.

-Notable Specimens:
1. Farga de Arion: Considered one of the oldest olive trees, with an estimated age of over 1,700 years. It is located in the municipality of Ulldecona, in Tarragona.
2. Olivo de Sinfo: Another millenary olive tree located in Traiguera, in the Valencian Community, estimated to be over 1,200 years old.

7

Spain is one of the world's leading wine producers, renowned for its diversity in wine regions, grape varieties, and wine styles.

Viticulture in Spain has a rich and ancient history, dating back over 3,000 years when the Phoenicians already cultivated vines on the Iberian Peninsula.

During Roman rule, Spanish wine gained importance and was exported throughout the Roman Empire.

In the 20th century, especially since the 1980s, there was a revival in the quality of Spanish wines due to the adoption of new winemaking techniques.

Among the prominent wine regions are:

-**Rioja:** Known for its red wines made from Tempranillo grapes.
-**Ribera del Duero:** Produces high-quality red wines, also primarily from Tempranillo grapes.
-**Jerez:** The birthplace of Sherry, known for its unique production and aging method called solera.
-**Priorat:** Famous for its powerful and complex reds, mainly made from Garnacha and Cariñena.
-**Rueda:** Recognized for its white wines made from Verdejo grapes.
-**Penedès:** One of the main sparkling wine (Cava) producing regions, though it also produces still wines.

Regarding grape varieties, Spain has a wide range, both red and white, including Tempranillo, Garnacha, Albariño, and Verdejo, among others.

The classification and regulation of Spanish wines are carried out through Denominations of Origin (DO) and Qualified Denominations of Origin (DOCa), a higher level awarded only to Rioja and Priorat.

Wine tourism is a growing attraction in Spain, with wine routes, wineries, and museums offering unique experiences for wine lovers.

8

The festival of San Fermín in Pamplona, Navarra, is one of the most famous and popular bullfighting festivals in the world.

This celebration, which includes the iconic running of the bulls, attracts thousands of visitors every year.

-History: The Sanfermines have their roots in the 12th century, when Saint Fermín, the patron saint of Navarra, was canonized. The modern celebrations that we know today date back to the 16th century. Originally, the festivities were held in October but were moved to July due to the better weather. The running of the bulls as we know it now began in the 19th century.

-Event Development: The festival is held annually from July 6th to 14th. The main activity is the running of the bulls, an 850-meter race that starts at 8:00 a.m., where the runners (mozos) try to stay ahead of a group of bulls until they reach the bullring. The festival officially starts with the launching of a rocket, known as chupinazo, from the balcony of the town hall. Besides the running of the bulls, there are parades with giant figures and big heads, religious processions, and other cultural events.

-Traditions and Characteristics: Participants usually wear white with a red neckerchief. Every afternoon, bullfights are held in the Pamplona bullring, one of the largest in Spain. The festivities culminate with the singing of Pobre de Mí on the night of July 14th, marking the official end of the celebrations.

-International Relevance: San Fermín attracts tourists from all over the world, who come to participate in or watch the running of the bulls. American writer Ernest Hemingway popularized the festival with his novel The Sun Also Rises, which helped draw international attention to the event.

-Controversies and Safety: Despite the safety measures, the running of the bulls remains a dangerous activity, and injuries occur every year.
The festival has been criticized by animal rights groups due to the bullfights and the use of animals in the running of the bulls.

San Fermín is one of Spain's most iconic festivals, a blend of tradition, excitement, and risk, reflecting the country's cultural richness and festive spirit.

9

Tapas are a culinary tradition deeply rooted in Spanish culture.

They refer to small portions of food that are commonly served as accompaniments to drinks in bars and restaurants.

-Origin and History: One popular version suggests that King Alfonso X "The Wise" ordered a small portion of food to be served with drinks to prevent people from drinking alcohol on an empty stomach. Another version indicates that a "tapa" (cover) was used to protect the contents of the drink glass from insects and dust, which led to the concept of serving some food on this cover. Initially, tapas consisted of basic foods like bread, cheese, and cold cuts, but over time, their variety and complexity have increased.

-Variety of Tapas:

1. Cold: Such as olives, cold cuts (ham, chorizo), cheeses, salads.
2. Hot: Spanish omelette, calamari, patatas bravas, croquettes.

Each region of Spain has its own varieties of tapas, such as gambas al ajillo in Andalusia, pintxos in the Basque Country, or patatas a la riojana in La Rioja.

-Tapas Culture: The act of going from bar to bar trying different tapas and drinks is a social way of eating that invites sharing and sampling a variety of flavors. In some regions, like Granada, it is common for tapas to be served for free when ordering a drink. In other places, like Madrid or Barcelona, they are usually charged.

- **Cultural Importance:** Tapas represent a social and relaxed lifestyle, where food is an excuse to share moments with friends and family. They are an important tourist attraction, as visitors want to experience this unique tradition.

- **Modern Evolution:** Tapas have evolved in modern cuisine, with chefs reinterpreting the classics in new and creative ways. The concept of tapas has transcended the borders of Spain and become a global phenomenon, with tapas bars present in many countries.

10

The legend of the werewolf has been part of Spanish mythology and folklore for centuries.

The figure of the werewolf is commonly associated with the transformation of a human into a wolf, either voluntarily or involuntarily, especially during the night of a full moon.

One of the best-known werewolf stories in Spain is that of the "Werewolf of Allariz."

According to legend, in the 18th century, in the Galician town of Allariz, there was a man named Manuel Blanco Romasanta, who earned his living as a traveling salesman.

He was accused of several crimes, including the murder of numerous people, and is believed to have transformed into a werewolf to commit his atrocities.

Another famous case is that of the "Werewolf of Cudillero," which took place in Asturias in the 19th century.

In this case, it was said that a man named Manuel Llana was believed to have the ability to transform into a wolf and attack livestock and locals.

These are just two examples of the many stories and legends of werewolves that have persisted in Spanish oral tradition over the years.

While there is no solid historical evidence to support the actual existence of werewolves, these stories have endured in popular culture and have inspired numerous works of literature, film, and television.

11

Spain is one of the world's most popular tourist destinations, attracting millions of visitors every year for its rich history, vibrant culture, geographical diversity, and favorable climate.

Spain is one of the world's most visited tourist destinations, with over 80 million international tourists annually, according to pre-COVID-19 pandemic figures.

Tourism is a fundamental part of the Spanish economy, representing approximately 12% of the country's GDP.

Main Destinations:

1. Cities:

-**Barcelona:** Famous for its modernist architecture, such as the Sagrada Familia and Park Güell, in addition to its beaches and nightlife.
-**Madrid:** The capital, with the Prado Museum, the Royal Palace, and the lively nightlife of neighborhoods like Malasaña and La Latina.
-**Seville:** With its Gothic cathedral, the Giralda, and the Royal Alcazar, and also the home of flamenco.
-**Granada:** Known for the Alhambra and its historic Albaicín neighborhood.
-**Valencia:** With its City of Arts and Sciences and the Fallas.

2. Coastal Regions:

-**Costa del Sol:** Popular for its beaches and warm climate, especially in places like Marbella and Malaga.
-**Balearic Islands:** Such as Mallorca, Menorca, and Ibiza, known for their beaches, landscapes, and nightlife.
-**Canary Islands:** They offer a subtropical climate year-round and unique volcanic landscapes.

3. Other Destinations:

- **Camino de Santiago:** A pilgrimage route that ends in Santiago de Compostela.
- **Pyrenees and Picos de Europa:** Destinations for nature and adventure tourism.

12

The Royal Palace of Madrid is the official residence of the King of Spain, though it is mainly used for official ceremonies and state functions.

-History and Architecture: The construction of the Royal Palace began in 1738 and was completed in 1764, during the reign of Charles III. It was built on the site of the old Alcázar, which was destroyed by a fire in 1734. The palace is designed in a Baroque style with Neoclassical influence and was designed by the architects Filippo Juvarra and, after his death, his disciple Giovanni Battista Sacchetti. It is the largest royal palace in Europe in terms of area, with approximately 135,000 square meters and over 3,000 rooms.

-Interiors and Collections: The palace has a series of impressive halls, such as the Throne Room, the Hall of Columns, and the Gala Dining Room. It houses an important art collection, including paintings by masters such as Caravaggio, Goya, and Velázquez. It also has a prominent collection of tapestries, furniture, and historical clocks. One of the palace's highlights is the Royal Armory, which contains a collection of weapons and armor from the 13th century onwards.

-Gardens and Exteriors: The Sabatini Gardens are located to the north of the palace and are known for their geometric design and fountains. Another royal garden, the Campo del Moro, located to the west of the palace, offers beautiful views of the building.

-Current Use: Although the king does not reside there, the Royal Palace is the monarch's official residence and is used for ceremonial events. It is open to the public in certain areas and is one of Madrid's most popular tourist destinations.

13

The Tabernas Desert is the only true desert in Europe and is located in the province of Almería, in southeastern Spain.

-Geographical and Climatic Features: It is situated between the Filabres and Alhamilla mountain ranges in the province of Almería. It has an arid climate, with temperatures that can exceed 40°C in summer and drop below 0°C in winter. Rainfall is very scarce, contributing to the area's aridity. The landscape is marked by vast plains, ravines, and rock formations eroded by wind and water, creating an environment similar to the deserts of the southwestern United States.

-History and Film: The Tabernas Desert became famous in the 1960s and 1970s when it was used as a set for numerous spaghetti westerns directed by filmmakers like Sergio Leone. Among the best-known films shot here are "The Good, the Bad and the Ugly" and "A Fistful of Dollars." As a result of its cinematic history, there are several theme parks and film studios in the desert that recreate Old West towns and movie sets.

-Flora and Fauna: Despite its aridity, the desert is home to a variety of resilient plants, such as esparto grass, thyme, and esparto. The fauna is also unique, with species adapted to extreme conditions, such as reptiles, birds, and some small mammals.

-Tourism: The desert is a popular destination for hikers and photographers due to its unique landscape. Guided tours of the theme parks and film sets are also available. Part of the desert is protected as the Tabernas Desert Natural Area, which helps preserve its flora, fauna, and landscape.

14

Spain has a rich cinematic tradition that has produced some of the most influential and internationally recognized directors.

-Pedro Almodóvar: Pedro Almodóvar began his career in the 1970s and became famous in the 1980s with films like "Women on the Verge of a Nervous Breakdown." His films are characterized by their focus on themes such as sexuality, desire, and identity, as well as a visually colorful and dramatic style. Among his most notable works are "All About My Mother," "Talk to Her," "Volver," and "Pain and Glory." He has won numerous awards, including two Academy Awards and several Goya Awards.

-Alejandro Amenábar: Of Chilean-Spanish descent, Alejandro Amenábar gained fame with "Thesis" in 1996 and has worked in both Spanish and Hollywood cinema. His films often contain elements of suspense, psychological thriller, and science fiction. Among his most notable works are "Open Your Eyes," "The Others," "The Sea Inside," and "Agora." He has won an Academy Award for "The Sea Inside" and several Goya Awards.

-Other Important Directors: Luis Buñuel is a pioneering figure of surrealist cinema and one of the most influential directors of the 20th century. His notable works include "The Exterminating Angel" and "Belle de Jour." Carlos Saura, known for his focus on social and cultural themes, has directed films like "Raise Ravens" and "Carmen." Víctor Erice, director of films such as "The Spirit of the Beehive" and "The South," is known for his poetic and visually beautiful approach.

-The Spanish Film Industry: Spain produces a significant number of films each year, ranging from drama and thriller to comedy. The San Sebastian International Film Festival is one of the most important festivals in Europe and the most prominent in Spain. In addition, Spain has a vibrant independent film scene, with festivals and awards dedicated to emerging filmmakers.

15

Bullrings in Spain have a deep historical and cultural tradition, although bullfighting is a controversial topic.

-History and Architecture: The first bullrings date back to the 18th century, although bullfighting goes back to earlier times when events were held in public squares. Bullrings are usually circular structures, allowing a complete view of the arena from any seat, and their design resembles Roman amphitheaters. Many bullrings have a neo-Mudéjar style, characterized by horseshoe arches and ceramic decorations.

-Famous Bullrings: The Las Ventas Bullring in Madrid is the largest bullring in Spain and one of the most iconic venues for bullfighting, with a capacity of over 23,000 people. The Maestranza Bullring in Seville is one of the oldest and is distinguished by its baroque style and historical significance. The Ronda Bullring, considered the cradle of modern bullfighting, is one of the oldest bullrings in Spain, with over two centuries of history. The Plaza Monumental in Barcelona, though no bullfights are held anymore in Catalonia, is one of the largest bullrings and has impressive architectural style.

-Cultural Importance: Bullrings symbolize a tradition that has been part of Spanish culture for centuries. In addition to being bullfighting venues, many are architectural monuments and are used for cultural events and concerts.

-Controversy and Legislation: Bullfighting is a controversial topic in Spain and abroad due to concerns about animal welfare, leading to protests and movements to ban bullfighting.
Some regions, such as Catalonia and the Canary Islands, have banned bullfighting, while others have declared it Intangible Cultural Heritage, legally protecting it.

-Current Use: Despite the controversy, bullfights remain popular in some regions of Spain, especially in the south and in Madrid. Additionally, many bullrings are used for concerts, shows, and tourist events, which helps maintain their cultural relevance.

16

The peseta was Spain's official currency before the euro was adopted in 2002.

-History of the Peseta: The peseta was introduced in 1868 during the reign of Isabel II, after Spain joined the Latin Monetary Union. It replaced various regional currencies to become the nation's official currency. The name "peseta" is believed to derive from "peso," a Spanish coin used in Latin America, and may also relate to the Catalan term "peceta," meaning "small piece."

-Features: Pesetas were issued in both coins and banknotes. The coins had denominations of 1, 5, 25, 50, 100, 200, and 500 pesetas, while the banknotes ranged from 100 to 10,000 pesetas. Both the coins and banknotes featured designs that reflected Spain's history and culture. The banknotes often depicted historical figures, while the coins included national symbols.

-Value and Parity: Throughout its history, the peseta experienced devaluations and inflation, impacting its value and purchasing power. In 1999, with the introduction of the euro, the peseta was officially replaced. The exchange rate was set at 166.386 pesetas per euro.

-Transition to the Euro: Between 1999 and 2002, the euro was introduced as an accounting currency, but the peseta continued to circulate physically until February 28, 2002, when it ceased to be legal tender. The adoption of the euro brought significant changes to Spain's financial and commercial landscape, and also affected people's perception of monetary value.

-Cultural Significance: For many, the peseta remains a nostalgic symbol of Spain's pre-euro economy. Pesetas have gained value as collectibles, especially those with specific designs or dates.

17

Spain is home to a variety of world-renowned museums that offer a unique perspective on history, art, and culture.

-Prado Museum: Located in Madrid, the Prado was founded in 1819 and houses one of the richest collections of European art, ranging from the 12th century to the early 20th century. It stands out for its extensive collection of works by artists such as Francisco de Goya, Diego Velázquez, El Greco, and Hieronymus Bosch. Notable works include Velázquez's "Las Meninas," Bosch's "The Garden of Earthly Delights," and Goya's "The Third of May 1808."

-Museo Nacional Centro de Arte Reina Sofía: Also located in Madrid, the Reina Sofía specializes in contemporary art. Founded in 1990, it houses a prominent collection of modern and contemporary art, including works by Pablo Picasso, Salvador Dalí, and Joan Miró. The museum's centerpiece is Picasso's "Guernica."

-Guggenheim Museum Bilbao: Located in Bilbao, this museum, inaugurated in 1997, is known for both its contemporary architecture and its collection. Designed by architect Frank Gehry, its exterior structure, with curved titanium panels, is an architectural landmark. It contains works by contemporary artists such as Jeff Koons, Louise Bourgeois, and Richard Serra.

-Thyssen-Bornemisza Museum: Located in Madrid, it complements the collections of the Prado and Reina Sofía. Opened to the public in 1992, it offers a journey through art from the Renaissance to the 20th century, with artists such as Dürer, Rubens, Van Gogh, Monet, and Hopper.

-Picasso Museum: With locations in Málaga and Barcelona, these museums contain a large collection of Pablo Picasso's works, from his early paintings to his more mature pieces. The one in Barcelona was founded in 1963, and the one in Málaga in 2003.

-Other Notable Museums: These include the National Art Museum of Catalonia (MNAC) in Barcelona, the Valencian Institute of Modern Art (IVAM) in Valencia, and the Museum of Spanish Abstract Art in Cuenca. These museums reflect Spain's rich artistic history and its commitment to preserving and promoting art on a global scale.

18

Spain is the birthplace of many important historical and cultural figures who have left a significant legacy in various fields.

-**Pablo Picasso:** Born in Málaga in 1881, Picasso was a painter, sculptor, and multidisciplinary artist. Considered one of the most influential artists of the 20th century, he is known for co-founding Cubism and innovating in Surrealism and other movements. Notable works include "Guernica," "Les Demoiselles d'Avignon," and "The Old Guitarist." His legacy endures in museums like the Picasso Museum in Barcelona and the Reina Sofía Museum.

-**Salvador Dalí:** Born in 1904 in Figueres, Dalí was a painter, sculptor, and filmmaker. Mainly associated with Surrealism, he was known for his extravagant style and dreamlike imagery. Notable works include "The Persistence of Memory," "The Great Masturbator," and "Swans Reflecting Elephants." The Dalí Theatre-Museum in Figueres is the main venue dedicated to his work.

-**Antoni Gaudí:** Born in 1852 in Reus, Gaudí was an architect. Considered the greatest exponent of Catalan modernism, his unique style integrates natural forms and organic designs. Notable works include the Sagrada Familia, Park Güell, and Casa Batlló. Many of his works are UNESCO World Heritage Sites.

-**Other Notable Figures:** It's worth mentioning Miguel de Cervantes, author of "Don Quixote," considered one of the most important works in world literature; Federico García Lorca, a poet and playwright, a main figure of the Generation of '27; Juan Ramón Jiménez, a poet and Nobel Prize winner in Literature, among many others.

19

There are various types of sharks along the Spanish coasts, differing in size, characteristics, and behavior.

1. Great White Shark (Carcharodon carcharias)
- **Size**: Up to 6 meters.
- **Characteristics**: Robust body, large triangular teeth. Gray on the back and white on the belly.
- **Aggressiveness**: Considered dangerous, but attacks are rare.
- **Locations**: Seen in the Mediterranean, near the coasts of Catalonia and the Balearic Islands.

2. Blue Shark (Prionace glauca)
- **Size**: Up to 3.8 meters.
- **Characteristics**: Slim body, bright blue on the back and white on the belly.
- **Aggressiveness**: Dangerous in specific situations, but rarely interacts with humans.
- **Locations**: Common in the Mediterranean and the Atlantic, especially around the Canary Islands.

3. Hammerhead Shark (Sphyrna spp.)
- **Size**: Up to 4 meters, depending on the species.
- **Characteristics**: Distinctive hammer-shaped head. Slim body and small teeth.
- **Aggressiveness**: Potentially dangerous, but not many incidents have been reported.
- **Locations**: Atlantic and Mediterranean, especially in deep waters.

4. Tope Shark (Galeorhinus galeus)
- **Size**: Up to 2 meters.
- **Characteristics**: Slender body and large eyes. Gray color.
- **Aggressiveness**: Not considered dangerous to humans.
- **Locations**: Found throughout the Atlantic and Mediterranean.

5. Basking Shark (Cetorhinus maximus)
- **Size:** Up to 10 meters.
- **Characteristics:** The second largest fish in the world. Feeds on plankton.
- **Aggressiveness:** Not dangerous to humans.
- **Locations:** Common in the North Atlantic, sometimes seen off the northern coast of Spain.

6. Shortfin Mako Shark (Isurus oxyrinchus)
- **Size:** Up to 4 meters.
- **Characteristics:** Streamlined body, sharp teeth.
- **Aggressiveness:** Potentially dangerous, but not commonly seen along the coast.
- **Locations:** Mainly in deep Atlantic waters.

7. Small-Spotted Catshark (Scyliorhinus canicula)
- **Size:** Up to 1 meter.
- **Characteristics:** Small shark, elongated body, brown spots.
- **Aggressiveness:** Not dangerous.
- **Locations:** Common throughout the Atlantic and Mediterranean.

8. Thresher Shark (Alopias vulpinus)
- **Size:** Up to 5 meters.
- **Characteristics:** Long tail used to stun prey.
- **Aggressiveness:** Not considered dangerous to humans.
- **Locations:** Mainly in the Atlantic, but also in the Mediterranean.

9. Sand Tiger Shark (Carcharias taurus)
- **Size:** Can reach 2 to 3 meters.
- **Characteristics:** Robust body, flattened head, and pointed teeth. Color varies between gray and brown, with a lighter belly.
- **Aggressiveness:** Despite its appearance, not considered very aggressive toward humans, but can be dangerous if provoked.
- **Locations:** Found in the Atlantic and, less frequently, in the Mediterranean, where it has been seen near the Andalusian coasts and in the Canary Islands. This shark prefers warm and temperate waters and is usually found in coastal areas and on continental shelves.

20

Spain is globally renowned for its rich and diverse culinary tradition.

-**Paella:** Originating from Valencia, a region in eastern Spain, paella is traditionally made with rice, seafood, rabbit, chicken, peppers, green beans, and saffron as the main spice. There are different types, such as Valencian paella (original with meat), seafood paella (only with seafood), and mixed paella (a combination of meat and seafood).

-**Spanish Tortilla:** Mainly made with eggs and potatoes, Spanish tortilla can also include onions, chorizo, spinach, or other ingredients. It's slowly cooked in a pan until it reaches a dense and juicy consistency. It's versatile and can be served hot or cold, as a tapa, sandwich, or main dish.

-**Gazpacho:** Originating from Andalusia in southern Spain, gazpacho is made with tomatoes, cucumbers, peppers, garlic, olive oil, vinegar, and bread. All ingredients are blended into a cold soup, perfect for hot days.

-**Other Famous Dishes:** Tapas are small portions of food served as an accompaniment to drinks and vary from olives and cold cuts to more elaborate dishes. Iberian ham, a cured ham from Iberian pigs, is considered a delicacy. Padrón peppers, some of which are spicy, are usually fried and sprinkled with salt. Galician-style octopus is made with boiled octopus, sliced and served with olive oil, paprika, and salt over potato slices. Fabada Asturiana is a stew from Asturias made with white beans, black pudding, chorizo, and pork belly. Cocido Madrileño is a traditional stew from Madrid made with chickpeas, meat, sausages, and vegetables. As a typical Catalan dessert, crema catalana is similar to the French crème brûlée.

-**General Characteristics of Spanish Cuisine:** Spanish cuisine is based on fresh ingredients like olive oil, vegetables, and fish, following the Mediterranean diet. Each region of Spain has its own culinary specialties, reflecting its geography and climate. Many Spanish dishes are still traditionally made, preserving the country's culinary heritage.

21

Mulhacén: The Highest Peak in the Iberian Peninsula.

-Geographical Features: At an elevation of 3,479 meters above sea level, Mulhacén dominates the Sierra Nevada National Park, located in the province of Granada. It is part of the Sierra Nevada mountain range, known for its rugged terrain and geological formations like slate and schist.

-Origin of the Name: The term "Mulhacén" originates from the Arabic "Mulay Hasan," which refers to the last Nasrid king of Granada, Muley Hacén. Although legend suggests he was buried at the summit, no archaeological evidence supports this.

-History and Cultural Significance: Surrounded by local legends and myths, Mulhacén has a mystical aura that has attracted explorers and naturalists since the 19th century. Its historical significance as a landmark has been crucial for early scientific expeditions in the region.

-Activities and Tourism: Mountaineering is a popular activity on Mulhacén, with hiking routes starting from towns like Capileira in the Alpujarra of Granada. While it isn't a ski resort, the nearby Sierra Nevada offers ski and snowboard slopes on other peaks.
The flora and fauna around Mulhacén are unique, with species adapted to the mountain's altitude and alpine climate.

-Climate: Due to its height, Mulhacén has an alpine climate, with temperatures dropping below zero for much of the year and permanent snow at the summit during the winter.

-Additional Facts: On clear days, the summit offers stunning views that include the African coast, the Mediterranean Sea, and vast expanses of the peninsula. Protected as part of the Sierra Nevada National Park, Mulhacén helps preserve the region's ecosystem and biodiversity.

22

The Canary Islands are renowned for their volcanic origin and the varied geological activity that has shaped their landscape over millions of years.

Mount Teide, on the island of Tenerife, stands out as one of the most iconic volcanoes.

-Mount Teide: At an altitude of 3,718 meters above sea level, Teide is the highest peak in Spain and the third highest volcano in the world from its base on the ocean floor. Located in Teide National Park on the island of Tenerife, Teide is still monitored for potential volcanic activity, although the last recorded eruption was in 1909, at a smaller vent nearby. For the Guanches, the indigenous people of the Canary Islands, Teide was a sacred place known as "Echeyde," which means "abode of the devil."

-Landscape and Ecosystem: Teide National Park showcases a landscape often compared to the lunar or Martian surface, with unique rock formations and lava fields. The climate conditions and altitude have allowed the evolution of endemic species like the red tajinaste and the black lizard.

-Other Volcanoes in the Canary Islands: Timanfaya, in Lanzarote, is famous for its lava fields and natural ovens, with its last major eruption occurring between 1730 and 1736. Cumbre Vieja, in La Palma, experienced recent activity in 2021, resulting in one of the most significant eruptions in recent decades. The Teneguía Volcano, also in La Palma, erupted in 1971, one of the last in the archipelago before Cumbre Vieja. Roque Nublo, in Gran Canaria, is a rock formation that originates as an ancient volcanic neck.

-Scientific and Touristic Importance: The Canary Islands attract the interest of volcanologists and scientists due to their volcanic activity and unique ecosystems. Tourism on the islands focuses on their national parks and protected areas, which receive millions of visitors each year interested in exploring their volcanic landscape, hiking, or simply enjoying the panoramic views.

23

Spain has been a fertile ground for the development of world-class tennis players, whose achievements have left an indelible mark on the sport.

-History and Development of Tennis in Spain: Tennis made its entry into Spain in the late 19th century, with tournaments held in select clubs. During the 1960s and 1970s, tennis began gaining popularity in the country, with figures like Manuel Santana and Andrés Gimeno paving the way for future generations.

-Rafael Nadal: Born in 1986 in Manacor, Mallorca, he has won multiple Grand Slam titles, notably with 14 titles at the French Open (Roland Garros). Known for his intensity, competitive mindset, and powerful forehand. Considered one of the greatest tennis players of all time, he has taken Spanish tennis to the top globally.

-Other Notable Spanish Tennis Players:
1. Manuel Santana, the first Spaniard to win Wimbledon in 1966, and also triumphed at the French Open and the U.S. Open.
2. Arantxa Sánchez Vicario, a multiple Grand Slam winner, especially at the French Open.
3. Conchita Martínez, the first Spanish woman to win Wimbledon in 1994.
4. Sergi Bruguera, a two-time consecutive winner at the French Open in 1993 and 1994.
5. Carlos Moyá, the French Open champion in 1998 and the first Spaniard to reach ATP world number 1.
6. Juan Carlos Ferrero, the French Open winner in 2003 and former world number 1.
7. Garbiñe Muguruza, winner of Wimbledon and the French Open, is one of Spain's leading current tennis players.

-Infrastructure and Development: Spain has a network of tennis academies and training centers, such as the Rafa Nadal Academy and the Sánchez-Casal Academy. The Mutua Madrid Open and the Barcelona Open are two of the country's most prestigious tournaments, attracting elite players from around the world. The Spanish Tennis Federation organizes and promotes the sport nationally, focusing on identifying and developing young talent.

24

Doñana National Park stands out as one of Europe's most important protected areas due to its diverse ecosystems and role as a refuge for endangered species.

-Location and Size: Located in southwestern Spain, it spans the provinces of Huelva, Seville, and Cádiz in the autonomous community of Andalusia. It covers more than 54,000 hectares, with an additional protected area, the Doñana Natural Park, adding another 54,000 hectares.

-History: Originally, the area was a private hunting estate known as Coto de Doñana. In 1969, it became a national park to safeguard its biodiversity. In 1980, UNESCO designated it a Biosphere Reserve, and in 1994 included it on the World Heritage List.

-Ecosystems: The park features a vast expanse of dunes, some of which are moving. The marshlands, flooded lands, are the main habitat for numerous waterfowl. The forests and scrublands provide shelter to a variety of mammal and bird species. It also has miles of pristine beaches.

-Biodiversity: Doñana is an important stopover for migratory birds between Europe and Africa, home to flamingos, Iberian imperial eagles, and many other species. It is known for housing endangered species like the Iberian lynx, the world's most threatened feline.
It's also a refuge for various species of reptiles and amphibians, many of which are endangered.

-Importance: The park is a living laboratory for the study of wetland ecosystems and their species. It attracts thousands of visitors each year for guided tours and birdwatching. It's one of the few places where marshlands and wetlands remain in their natural state.

-Threats and Challenges: Urbanization in the surrounding areas poses threats to the park. The intensive use of water for agriculture and other activities has affected the water level in the marshlands.
Climate change is impacting migration patterns and water availability.

25

Toledo and Seville boast a rich historical legacy as former capitals of the Kingdom of Spain, each standing out in different eras and reflecting the power and culture of their time.

Toledo, during the Visigothic period, became the capital of the Visigothic Kingdom in the 6th century after the fall of the Roman Empire, serving as a political and religious center until the Muslim invasion.

The Reconquista returned it to Christian hands in 1085, making it the capital of the Kingdom of Castile until the 16th century.

During the reign of Charles I, Toledo was the capital of the Spanish Empire.

Additionally, it has been a prominent religious center as the seat of the Primatial Archbishopric of Spain.

Its cultural heritage is evident as "the city of three cultures," due to the historical coexistence of Christians, Jews, and Muslims, visible in the cathedral, the Alcázar, and the Jewish quarter.

Seville, under Islamic rule as Isbiliya, stood out particularly during the Caliphate of Córdoba and the Taifa kingdom.

Ferdinand III of Castile reconquered it in 1248, turning it into a Christian city.

It became the capital of trade with the New World after the discovery of America in 1492, with the establishment of the House of Trade to manage trade between Spain and the American colonies.

During the Renaissance and the Golden Age, Seville flourished as one of the most important cities in Europe, reflecting its wealth in its buildings and culture.

Its cultural heritage, with the Royal Alcázar, the Seville Cathedral, and the Giralda, is a testament to its vast history and the mix of architectural styles.

Both historic centers have been declared UNESCO World Heritage Sites, a recognition of their historical and cultural importance.

Toledo and Seville remain significant cultural centers in Spain, attracting tourists and serving as symbols of the country's historical past.

They represent crucial periods in Spanish history, whose architecture, art, and history reflect the political and cultural changes over the centuries.

26

Ratoncito Pérez is a well-established figure in Spanish children's culture and in other Spanish-speaking countries.

Its origins date back to 1894 when Jesuit priest Luis Coloma created the character by writing a story titled "Ratón Pérez" for young King Alfonso XIII, who had lost a tooth at the age of eight.

In the original story, Ratoncito Pérez resides in a cookie box inside a confectionery in Madrid.

When King Buby (the name used for Alfonso XIII in the story) loses a tooth, the little mouse visits him and leaves a coin.

The figure of Ratoncito Pérez is part of a deep-rooted tradition where, like the Tooth Fairy, he is said to visit children at night, collecting their fallen teeth from under the pillow and leaving a coin or a small gift in their place.

Although Luis Coloma is recognized as the creator of the character, the notion of a creature that exchanges teeth for coins has roots in ancient legends and oral traditions, varying from country to country.

Today, Ratoncito Pérez's presence remains alive in popular culture.

In Madrid, near the place where Coloma imagined his home, there is a small museum dedicated to the character, along with sculptures and references in other cities.

Furthermore, Ratoncito Pérez has been adapted on numerous occasions, from television programs to books and movies, which has helped maintain his popularity.

This endearing character not only symbolizes the transition from childhood to adolescence but also the importance of dental care.

For many children, receiving a coin in exchange for a fallen tooth represents a significant rite of passage.

Its cultural influence has transcended Spain's borders and is widely known in most Spanish-speaking countries.

27

The Lady of Elche is one of Spain's most famous archaeological pieces and a symbol of Iberian art.

It is estimated that this sculpture was carved in the 4th century BC and was discovered in 1897 by a farmer named Manuel Campello at a site known as La Alcudia, near Elche in the province of Alicante.

After its discovery, the sculpture was sold to the Louvre in Paris, where it remained until 1941, when it was returned to Spain.

The Lady of Elche, carved from limestone, has approximate dimensions of 56 centimeters in height and weighs around 65 kilograms.

The figure depicts a woman with an elaborate headdress and ear and neck ornaments, suggesting a high social status.

Its style shows influences from various Mediterranean cultures, particularly Greek and Phoenician.

There are various interpretations of its meaning: some researchers believe it might represent an Iberian goddess or priestess due to the religious significance of female sculptures in ancient cultures, while others suggest it may have been a funerary vessel, given the discovery of cavities in the back that might have contained ashes.

The Lady of Elche is a valuable example of Iberian art and reflects the sophistication of this pre-Roman civilization.

It has become a national cultural symbol, being the subject of numerous reproductions and references in popular culture.

Currently, the sculpture is on display at the National Archaeological Museum of Spain in Madrid, although replicas can also be found in other museums and locations, such as the Archaeological and History Museum of Elche, near the site of its original discovery.

28

Las Fallas are one of Spain's largest and most iconic festivals, celebrated in the city of Valencia and other towns in the Valencian Community.

With roots in a medieval tradition where carpenters burned their old tools on the eve of St. Joseph's Day, Las Fallas have evolved into artistic monuments that depict satirical scenes of society.

These monuments, known as "fallas," are large constructions made of flammable materials such as cardboard, wood, and cork, with some reaching heights of over 20 meters.

The figures that make up the fallas, called "ninots," often represent famous characters, politicians, or humorous scenes.

The act of setting up these monuments on the streets, called the "plantà," marks the official start of the festivities.

During Las Fallas, various traditions take place, such as the "mascletà," a pyrotechnic display that takes place every day at 2:00 p.m., and the flower offering to the Virgin of the Forsaken, patroness of Valencia, which creates an impressive flower mantle.

The highlight of Las Fallas is the night of March 19, when all the fallas are burned in huge bonfires, an event known as the "Cremà."

However, one ninot is saved by popular vote and displayed in the Fallas Museum.

Las Fallas are organized by fallas commissions, groups of neighbors who handle the construction of the fallas and the organization of the festivities.

During the celebration, the "falleros" and "falleras" wear traditional Valencian costumes.

In 2016, Las Fallas were declared an Intangible Cultural Heritage of Humanity by UNESCO, which highlights their cultural importance and value as a unique event that attracts thousands of national and international tourists.

Known for their humorous critique of society, politics, and culture, Las Fallas also showcase the artistic creativity of the "falleros" artists, who work throughout the year to create these impressive structures.

29

The "Cantar de mio Cid" is one of the most emblematic works of medieval Spanish literature and represents one of the earliest examples of written Castilian.

It is estimated to have been written around 1200 by an anonymous author, although some scholars suggest it may have been composed by a minstrel with historical knowledge.

The poem recounts the exploits of the knight Rodrigo Díaz de Vivar, known as El Cid Campeador, who lived in the 11th century.

It focuses on his exile, his battles to restore his honor, and the eventual restoration of his position.

It is divided into three parts, or "cantares": the "Cantar del destierro," the "Cantar de las bodas," and the "Cantar de la afrenta de Corpes," which narrate different aspects of El Cid's life.

The "Cantar de mio Cid" is one of the oldest surviving texts in Castilian and an early example of epic verse in Spanish literature.

Although it includes legendary elements, many of the events and characters are based on real events and people, giving it significant historical value.

Moreover, it is considered a gem of Spanish literary heritage and an important source for the study of medieval language and culture.

Medieval Castilian developed from Vulgar Latin in the region of Castile during the early Middle Ages.

It differs significantly from modern Spanish in terms of verb forms, vocabulary, and spelling.

Apart from the "Cantar de mio Cid," other important texts in medieval Castilian include Alfonso X's "Siete Partidas" and the works of the Archpriest of Hita.

The oldest manuscript of the "Cantar de mio Cid" is preserved in the National Library of Spain, being a 14th-century copy.

This suggests that the work was transmitted orally for a long time before being put into writing.

It has been the subject of numerous critical studies that attempt to understand its historical, literary, and linguistic context.

30

Primavera Sound is a music festival held annually in Barcelona.

Founded in 2001, it has become one of the most important and recognized festivals in Europe, attracting thousands of attendees from around the world.

-History and Foundation: Primavera Sound was founded in 2001 by a team of young music enthusiasts. Since then, it has seen considerable growth in both size and reputation.

-Location: The festival takes place at Parc del Fòrum, a public space near the Mediterranean Sea in Barcelona. In addition to the main concerts, the festival also includes events at other venues in the city.

-Musical Variety: Primavera Sound stands out for its eclectic selection of artists and musical genres. From indie rock to electronic, hip-hop, pop, punk, and more, the festival offers a wide range of performances to suit all tastes.

-International Stage: Over the years, Primavera Sound has featured many world-renowned artists as well as emerging talent. These include bands and artists like Radiohead, Björk, Arcade Fire, Kendrick Lamar, The Strokes, and many more.

-Atmosphere and Experience: In addition to the music, the festival offers a unique experience, with a vibrant festival atmosphere. Attendees can enjoy a wide variety of activities, including food and drink areas, craft markets, and art spaces.

-Innovation and Sustainability: Primavera Sound has shown a commitment to innovation and sustainability. For example, it has implemented measures to reduce its carbon footprint and promote environmentally responsible practices.

-Programming and Schedule: The festival extends over several days, with performances generally starting in the afternoon and continuing until the early morning hours. The full schedule is announced in advance, allowing attendees to plan their agenda and make the most of the experience.

31

Historical Figures of the Iberian Peninsula in Ancient Times

-Lucius Cornelius Balbus the Elder: Originally from Gades (modern-day Cádiz), he was a general and politician who became a Roman citizen. He was close to Julius Caesar and rose to power, becoming the first non-Roman to hold the position of consul in Rome.

-Himilco: A Carthaginian navigator, possibly originating from the southern region of the Iberian Peninsula, known for his exploration voyages in the Atlantic Ocean.

-Viriathus: A Lusitanian leader who led the resistance against Roman conquest in the 2nd century BC. Known for his military cunning and charisma, he was a central figure in the Lusitanian Wars.

-Trajan: Born in Italica (near present-day Seville), he was the first Roman emperor of Hispanic origin. He ruled from 98 AD to 117 AD and is known for expanding the Roman Empire to its greatest extent.

-Hadrian: Nephew of Trajan, he was also born in Italica and was a Roman emperor from 117 AD to 138 AD. He was known for his administrative reforms and the construction of Hadrian's Wall in Britain.

-Lucius Annaeus Seneca: Born in Córdoba, he was a Stoic philosopher, writer, and Roman statesman. He was an advisor to Emperor Nero and is known for his philosophical and literary work.

-Martial: Born in Bilbilis (near present-day Calatayud), he was a Roman poet famous for his satirical epigrams that offer a glimpse into life in ancient Rome.

-Theodosius I the Great: He was the last emperor to rule the unified Roman Empire before its division. Although born in Cauca (Coca, Segovia), in present-day Spain, his father, Theodosius the Elder, was also a notable Roman military leader.

32

Mérida, a city located in the autonomous community of Extremadura in southwestern Spain, was known as Augusta Emerita in Roman times.

It was founded in 25 BC by order of Emperor Augustus as a colony for the veterans of the Roman legions.

The city is famous for having some of the best-preserved Roman ruins on the Iberian Peninsula, including its impressive Roman theater.

The Roman theater of Mérida was built between 16 BC and 15 BC and is considered one of the best-preserved theaters in all of Hispania, the Roman province that encompassed much of present-day Spain and Portugal.

This theater was designed to accommodate up to 6,000 spectators and was the epicenter of theatrical and cultural events during Roman times.

The theater is part of the Archaeological Ensemble of Mérida, which includes other notable Roman monuments such as the Amphitheater, the Roman Circus, the Temple of Diana, and the Aqueduct of Los Milagros.

The entire ensemble was declared a UNESCO World Heritage Site in 1993, in recognition of its exceptional state of preservation and historical significance.

Today, the theater remains an active venue, hosting modern cultural events like the Mérida International Classical Theater Festival, a testament to the incredible longevity and historical relevance of this site.

33

The Route of Don Quixote is a cultural tourist itinerary that follows in the footsteps of the famous literary character Don Quixote, created by Miguel de Cervantes in his work "The Ingenious Gentleman Don Quixote of La Mancha."

This itinerary crosses Castilla-La Mancha, the region where Cervantes set the adventures of Don Quixote and his loyal squire, Sancho Panza.

The route covers places that inspired key episodes in the novel.

Some highlights include:

-**Alcalá de Henares:** Although not part of Don Quixote's classic route, it is the birthplace of Cervantes.

-**Toledo:** The capital of Castilla-La Mancha and a place where Cervantes found inspiration.

-**Consuegra:** Known for its windmills, an iconic symbol of fighting "giants" in the novel.

-**El Toboso:** The home of Dulcinea, Don Quixote's platonic love.

-**Campo de Criptana:** Famous for its windmills, which many associate with Don Quixote's famous battle.

-**Argamasilla de Alba:** Where, according to tradition, Cervantes began writing the book while imprisoned.

-**Puerto Lápice:** The place where Don Quixote was knighted.

The Route of Don Quixote allows visitors to explore the culture, landscape, and history of the region, offering a deeper experience of the novel's meaning and impact.

"Don Quixote," first published in 1605 (first part) and 1615 (second part), is a literary work that addresses universal themes such as idealism, honor, and madness.

34

Spain is known for its varied coastal geography, ranging from white sandy beaches and crystal-clear waters in the Mediterranean to rugged and wild shores on the Atlantic.

-**Playa del Silencio, Asturias:** Located on the northern coast, this beach is also known as El Gavieiru. It is one of the most stunning beaches in Asturias, famous for its limestone cliffs and its quiet, secluded atmosphere. It has no facilities or services, which adds to its pristine, natural atmosphere.

-**Playa de Ses Illetes, Formentera:** Located on the small island of Formentera, this white sandy beach with turquoise waters is famous for its natural beauty. It has been compared to Caribbean beaches.

-**Playa de La Concha, San Sebastián:** Located in the Basque Country, it is one of the most well-known urban beaches in the country. Its shell shape, fine sand, and panoramic views make it an iconic destination.

-**Playa de Las Catedrales, Galicia:** Famous for its impressive rock formations, which are accessible only at low tide. The rock walls resemble cathedrals, hence the name.

-**Playa de Bolonia, Cádiz:** A vast, untouched beach with views of the Strait of Gibraltar. The Roman ruins of Baelo Claudia are nearby.

-**Playa de la Cala Macarella, Menorca:** A small cove on the island of Menorca, famous for its turquoise waters and white sand. It is surrounded by high cliffs and pine forests.

-**Playa de Maspalomas, Gran Canaria:** Famous for its enormous sand dunes that resemble a miniature desert. The beach is ideal for walks and enjoying the Atlantic Ocean.

These beaches reflect the diversity of Spain's coasts, offering something for every type of traveler.

35

The National Museum of Roman Art (MNAR) in Mérida is a key institution for the study and exhibition of Roman art on the Iberian Peninsula.

Founded in 1986, the museum is located near the Roman ruins of the ancient Augusta Emerita, making it an ideal place to showcase its collection.

The MNAR houses one of the largest collections of Roman mosaics in Spain and the world.

Roman mosaics are a form of decorative art created by the Romans, using small fragments of stone, glass, or ceramic to create detailed images that decorated floors and walls.

The mosaics displayed in the museum come primarily from local archaeological sites, allowing visitors to gain an authentic insight into the interiors of Roman houses and buildings in Augusta Emerita.

Highlighted Features of the MNAR Mosaics:

-Themes: The mosaics feature a variety of themes, from mythological scenes and human figures to geometric and natural motifs like plants and animals.

-Techniques: Many of the mosaics are made using the "opus tessellatum" technique, using small squares of stone and glass to create detailed images. Some examples also use "opus vermiculatum," a finer technique that allows for greater detail.

-State of Conservation: Many of the mosaics are well-preserved, allowing the original details and colors to be appreciated.
Importance:

The MNAR's mosaic collection provides important insight into the art and life of ancient Augusta Emerita.

The mosaics offer information about the beliefs, aesthetics, and daily life of Roman society.

Additionally, the museum uses these works to educate the public about Mérida's history and its relevance in the context of Roman Hispania.

36

The Alhambra, located in Granada, is a monumental complex from the Muslim era and one of the most iconic tourist destinations in the country.

Its construction began in the 13th century during the Nasrid Kingdom and served as a palace and fortress for the Nasrid monarchs and their court.

Famous for its impressive Islamic architecture, the Alhambra is distinguished by its intricate decorative details, colorful tiles, wooden ceilings, elaborate plasterwork, and gardens with fountains.

Its architectural style combines Islamic art with later Christian influences.

Recognized as a UNESCO World Heritage Site in 1984, along with the Generalife and the Albaicín, the Alhambra is prized for its historical and cultural significance.

Among its main attractions are the Palace of the Nasrid, the Palace of Charles V, the Generalife, the Alcazaba, and other notable structures, each with its own unique history and features.

The Alhambra has been a source of inspiration for artists, writers, and musicians for centuries, symbolizing the encounter between Islamic and Christian cultures in Spain's history.

As the most visited monument in the country, it attracts millions of tourists every year, with tickets often selling out weeks in advance due to its immense popularity.

37

The Festival of Lights of Arcos de la Frontera, also known as the Zambomba de Arcos or "Arcos in the Light of Candles," is a cultural event that takes place in December in this charming town in the province of Cádiz, in the region of Andalusia.

This festival, held in the old town of Arcos de la Frontera, is known for its picturesque beauty and its roots in Andalusian Christmas traditions.

One of the festival's most notable features is the candle lighting that transforms the town's streets, balconies, and squares into a magical and unique setting.

This atmosphere is complemented by a variety of musical performances, with special emphasis on the zambomba, a traditional Andalusian Christmas music.

Additionally, you can enjoy Christmas carols, dance performances, and other shows in different parts of the town.

The event also offers the opportunity to explore local crafts and enjoy traditional cuisine, with craft markets and food stalls offering local products and typical sweets of the Christmas season.

The active participation of the local community in organizing the festival adds a sense of authenticity and warmth, as residents come together to decorate the streets and organize activities.

Overall, the Festival of Lights of Arcos de la Frontera blends the historical charm of the town with vibrant Andalusian Christmas traditions, creating an unforgettable experience for both locals and visitors.

38

The Galician rías are unique and distinctive geographical formations in the region of Galicia, in northwestern Spain.

These estuaries were formed by the sinking of river valleys due to the rising sea level, resulting in coastal inlets that fill with seawater and mix with fresh river water, creating a unique and highly productive environment.

They are mainly classified into two groups: the Rías Altas, located in the north, such as the Ría de Ferrol, Ría de Ortigueira, and Ría de Viveiro, which are smaller and shallower; and the Rías Baixas, in the south, such as the Ría de Vigo, Ría de Arousa, and Ría de Pontevedra, which are larger, deeper, and have more open landscapes.

These rías are rich in marine biodiversity due to the mixing of fresh and saltwater, as well as the geological and climatic features of the area, making them one of the most productive ecosystems for the cultivation and fishing of shellfish such as mussels, oysters, and clams.

In addition to their biodiversity, the rías offer spectacular landscapes, with fine sandy beaches, cliffs, islands, and lush vegetation, making them popular tourist destinations.

Their appeal is not limited to their natural beauty, but also includes their cultural and gastronomic richness, renowned for their delicious cuisine, especially fresh seafood.

Dishes like Galician-style octopus, boiled seafood, and empanadas are local specialties.

Fishing and aquaculture are important economic pillars in the region, thanks to the abundance of marine resources in the rías.

In addition, related industries such as fish canning contribute significantly to the local economy.

39

The legacy of Francisco Franco, the Spanish dictator who ruled from 1939 until his death in 1975, remains a topic of debate and controversy in Spain.

After Franco's death, and especially after the transition to democracy, many statues and monuments of the dictator were removed or relocated.

However, some remain, generating debates about their significance and place in Spanish history.

One of the most controversial is the Valley of the Fallen, a monument built under Franco's regime that housed his tomb (until his exhumation in 2019) and those of others who died during the Civil War.

This place is especially controversial due to its symbolism and origin, as it was largely built with forced labor from political prisoners.

In 2007, Spain passed the Historical Memory Law aimed at eliminating symbols and monuments that glorified the Franco regime.

This led to the removal of many statues and street names related to Franco. However, the process has been slow and sometimes contentious.

The issue of the remnants of Francoism remains hotly debated today.

While some sectors advocate for the complete removal of any regime symbols, others believe some should be preserved as historical reminders.

This debate is tied to how Spain confronts its recent past, seeking a balance between remembering the victims of the dictatorship and avoiding extreme polarization in today's society, thereby promoting historical memory and reconciliation.

40

Spanish Superstitions: A Reflection of History and Cultural Syncretism.

-Tuesday the 13th: In Spain, Tuesday the 13th is considered an unlucky day, similar to Friday the 13th in many Western cultures. This is believed to stem from the combination of the number 13, considered unlucky in many cultures, and Tuesday, a day associated with the Roman god Mars, who symbolizes war and conflict.

-Walking Under a Ladder: Similar to other cultures, walking under a ladder is considered bad luck in Spain. This may be related to the belief that it forms a triangle, a sacred symbol that shouldn't be desecrated.

-Spilling Salt: Spilling salt is also considered bad luck. To counteract this, it's advised to take a pinch of salt and throw it over the left shoulder.

-Horseshoe: The horseshoe is a symbol of good luck in Spain, as in many other cultures. It's believed to bring protection and good fortune, and it's common to find it on house doors.

-Black Cats: In Spain, black cats are associated with bad luck, a superstition shared with many other Western cultures.

-Knock on Wood: The phrase "knock on wood" is commonly used to avoid bad luck. People touch any nearby wooden object while saying it to ward off misfortune.

-Garlic to Ward Off Evil: Garlic has historically been used as an amulet to ward off evil spirits and protect against the evil eye.

-Open Scissors: Leaving scissors open is considered bad luck, as it symbolizes a cut in relationships or conflicts.

-Sweeping Feet: If someone accidentally sweeps another person's feet, it's said that person will never get married.

-Starting with the Right Foot: It's believed that starting the day by putting on the right shoe first or starting with the right foot brings good luck.

41

The siesta is a widely known Spanish tradition that involves a short rest or nap after lunch.

Although it's a stereotype associated with Spain, it is still practiced in many parts of the country.

The siesta has its roots in Mediterranean culture and dates back to Roman times. The word "siesta" comes from the Latin "sexta hora," which means the sixth hour of the day, around noon.

Traditionally, the siesta was taken to avoid the hottest hours of the day and to make the best use of time.

In agricultural areas, it was also a time to rest before returning to fieldwork.

The siesta traditionally lasts between 15 and 30 minutes, although some people may take longer naps.

It usually takes place after lunch, around noon or early afternoon.

Scientific studies suggest that short naps can improve alertness, cognitive performance, and mood.

They help combat drowsiness and may reduce the risk of cardiovascular diseases.

Modern lifestyles have affected the practice of the siesta in Spain.

In big cities, where work schedules are stricter, it's less common to find time for a siesta, although in small towns and on weekends, it's more likely to find people who maintain this tradition.

Despite its decline, the siesta remains an important part of Spanish culture and a symbol of the relaxed lifestyle associated with the Mediterranean region.

The siesta is more than a tradition; it's a cultural symbol that reflects a different approach to the balance between work and rest.

42

"Olé" is a widely used expression in Spain, particularly in contexts related to flamenco, bullfighting, and other cultural celebrations.

Although the exact origin of "olé" is not entirely clear, it is believed to come from the Arabic "Allah," meaning "God."

This expression may have been adapted by the Spanish during the Muslim rule of the Iberian Peninsula.

In flamenco, "olé" is commonly used to express admiration and enthusiasm.

Spectators use it to show appreciation for an especially emotional or technically skilled performance by singers, musicians, or dancers.

In bullfighting, "olé" is used to praise a good move by the bullfighter or a well-executed pass during the fight.

It is a gesture of recognition for the bullfighter's skill and courage.

Beyond flamenco and bullfighting, "olé" is also used in other contexts to express approval, enthusiasm, and jubilation at popular festivals, sporting events, and other celebrations.

"Olé" is more than an expression; it is a symbol of Spanish enthusiasm and passion, reflecting the vibrant spirit and energy of the country's culture.

In short, "olé" is a word filled with emotion that has endured for centuries as a symbol of admiration and passion in various art forms and cultural events in Spain.

43

The Hermida Gorge is an impressive geographical formation located in Cantabria, an autonomous community in northern Spain.

Located in the heart of Cantabria, between the municipalities of Potes and Peñarrubia, the Hermida Gorge is the main entrance to the Liébana Valley and serves as the gateway to the Picos de Europa, one of Spain's most impressive mountain ranges.

With a length of approximately 21 kilometers, it is the longest gorge in Spain.

It is carved by the Deva River, which has created limestone walls that can reach up to 600 meters in height.

The gorge offers spectacular landscapes and great biodiversity.

The steep slopes are covered with varied vegetation and are home to animal species like birds of prey.

Moreover, the Deva River is a habitat for aquatic species like trout.

It's a popular destination for nature lovers and outdoor activities.

You can enjoy hiking, climbing, and birdwatching.

There are also scenic routes for those who prefer to explore by car.

Since ancient times, it has been an important communication route, connecting the Liébana Valley with the rest of Cantabria.

The Camino Lebaniego, a pilgrimage route linking the Camino de Santiago with the Monastery of Santo Toribio de Liébana, passes through here.

Near the gorge, in the municipality of La Hermida, are the thermal baths of the La Hermida Spa, known for their mineral-medicinal waters.

44

dioms and popular sayings reflect a country's culture and traditional wisdom.

-Don't look a gift horse in the mouth: Appreciate what you are given without focusing on negative details. It refers to gratitude for a gift.

-Better late than never: It's better to do something late than never to do it at all.

-Silence is golden: Sometimes it's better to keep quiet to avoid getting into trouble.

-Raise crows, and they'll gouge out your eyes: If you help ungrateful people, they may turn against you.

-Play dumb: Pretend not to understand something to avoid doing something or answering a question.

-The early bird catches the worm: People who put in the effort early in life or in a project tend to be more successful.

-Head in the clouds: To be distracted or not pay attention to what's happening.

-Every cloud has a silver lining: Something positive can come from bad situations.

-To spend an arm and a leg: To spend a lot of money on something, usually for a special occasion.

-To be the last straw: To be the least important person in a group or organization.

- **There's no one more blind than those who refuse to see:** Those who deliberately ignore the truth are the most stubborn.

- **Like father, like son:** Children often resemble their parents, both in appearance and character.

- **A word to the wise is enough:** An intelligent person understands things without the need for long explanations.

- **Hold the reins:** To have control of a situation.
Kill two birds with one stone: Achieve two goals with one action.

- **A bird in the hand is worth two in the bush:** It's better to have something certain, even if it's little, than risk losing it for something uncertain.

- **Between a rock and a hard place:** To be in a difficult situation with no good way out.

- **Get to the point:** Go straight to the main issue, without beating around the bush.

- **Everyone makes mistakes:** Everyone makes mistakes, especially when speaking.

- **Pull yourself together:** Start working or studying with more energy and efficiency.

45

The original name of Spain traces back to the word Hispania, used by the ancient Romans to refer to the Iberian Peninsula.

There are several theories about the origin of the name Hispania:

-Phoenician: The most accepted theory is that it comes from the Phoenician word i-shphanim, meaning "land of rabbits," in reference to the abundance of these animals on the peninsula.

-Greek: Another theory suggests that it derives from the Greek name Hispalis, which the Greeks used to refer to the peninsula.

-Iberian: Some scholars believe the name might have roots in the Iberian language, a non-Indo-European language spoken on the peninsula.

-Latin: Finally, the Roman version was adapted to Hispania, a name the Romans used to designate the region after conquering it.

The transformation from Hispania to Spain occurred gradually over the centuries.

During the Middle Ages, the name transformed to Spain, mainly through Vulgar Latin and the Castilian language, partly due to the influence of the Visigoths and later the Reconquista, which united the Christian kingdoms in the fight against the Muslims.

In the 15th century, with the union of the Catholic Monarchs, Ferdinand of Aragon and Isabella of Castile, and the unification of the Christian kingdoms under one crown, the name Spain began to be used more widely to refer to the entire territory, consolidating into its current form and becoming the official name of the country.

46

**Salamanca is famous for its historic university,
one of the oldest in Europe and the world.**

The University of Salamanca was founded in 1218 by King Alfonso IX of León, becoming one of the first universities to receive royal status.

Its prestige and historical influence rank it among the most important universities in Europe.

During the Middle Ages and the Renaissance, the University of Salamanca was a renowned center of learning, compared to the universities of Oxford and Bologna.

It was a hub of humanism and canon law, influencing the development of knowledge in Europe.

The university has been a cradle for important figures such as the Dominican friar Francisco de Vitoria, one of the founders of international law, and Miguel de Unamuno, a 20th-century philosopher and writer.

The university's historic building, with its Plateresque facade, is one of Salamanca's most iconic landmarks.

Other notable buildings include the Escuelas Mayores, the Escuelas Menores, and the Patio de Escuelas.

The presence of students has shaped Salamanca's culture for centuries.

Today, the university has tens of thousands of students, including many international students.

Salamanca's historic center was declared a UNESCO World Heritage Site in 1988, partly due to its university legacy.

The city hosts cultural events, conferences, and academic activities that attract people from all over the world.

The student atmosphere creates a vibrant vibe in the city.

The University of Salamanca and the city as a whole are living witnesses of the history of education and culture in Europe, representing a legacy that has endured for over 800 years.

47

Schedules in Spain tend to differ from those in many other countries, especially regarding meals and daily activities.

-Lunch Schedule: Lunch, the main meal of the day in Spain, usually takes place between 2:00 p.m. and 4:00 p.m. This is noticeably later than in other European countries. Many companies offer a break of several hours so employees can enjoy a long meal and, in some areas, even a siesta.

-Dinner Schedule: Dinner in Spain is lighter than lunch and is usually served after 9:00 p.m., reaching even 11:00 p.m. in some regions. This is partly due to the custom of having tapas or appetizers in bars before dinner.

-Work Hours: Companies usually start their workday between 9:00 a.m. and 10:00 a.m., and many have a long lunch break, resuming activities in the afternoon and working until 8:00 p.m.

-Store Hours: Stores generally open from 10:00 a.m. to 2:00 p.m. and from 5:00 p.m. to 8:00 p.m. or 9:00 p.m. However, in tourist areas and large cities, many stores remain open all day.

-School Hours: Schools usually start around 9:00 a.m. and finish around 2:00 p.m. Some schools offer afternoon classes, but it is not as common.

-Leisure and Nightlife Hours: Nightlife in Spain usually starts late. Bars can fill up from 11:00 p.m., and clubs do not get lively until after midnight, staying open until the early hours of the morning.

-Historical Reasons: Spanish schedules reflect historical, geographical, and cultural factors. During the Civil War and the Franco dictatorship, work schedules were adapted to make the most of daylight hours. Additionally, the adoption of Central European Time instead of Greenwich Mean Time, which is more natural for Spain, has also contributed to this time difference.

48

The conquest history of Spain in the 15th century is an important milestone in world history, marking the beginning of the European age of exploration and colonization in the New World.

-**Catholic Monarchs:** Isabella I of Castile and Ferdinand II of Aragon, known as the Catholic Monarchs, unified the kingdoms of Castile and Aragon through their marriage. Their reign represented the unification of much of the Iberian Peninsula, and together they promoted the expansion and consolidation of the Spanish monarchy.

-**Christopher Columbus and the Discovery of America:** In 1492, Christopher Columbus, financed by the Catholic Monarchs, embarked on a journey westward to find a new route to the Indies. Instead, he discovered America, though he thought he had reached Asia. This event marked the beginning of Spain's era of conquest and colonization of the New World.

-**Treaty of Tordesillas:** In 1494, the Treaty of Tordesillas was signed between Spain and Portugal, dividing the newly discovered New World between the two countries through an imaginary line. This allowed Spain to claim most of the American continent, excluding Brazil, which remained under Portuguese control.

-**Conquistadors and Colonization:** During the 16th century, conquistadors like Hernán Cortés and Francisco Pizarro expanded Spanish control over large indigenous empires, such as the Aztec Empire in Mexico and the Inca Empire in Peru. This period was marked by brutality, exploitation, and a devastating cultural and demographic impact on the indigenous populations.

-**Viceroyalties:** The Spanish crown established viceroyalties to administer the vast conquered territories. The Viceroyalty of New Spain (present-day Mexico and Central America) and the Viceroyalty of Peru were the most important.

-**Columbian Exchange:** The discovery of America initiated the exchange of plants, animals, diseases, and cultures between the Old and New Worlds. This is known as the Columbian Exchange, which had a lasting impact on world history.

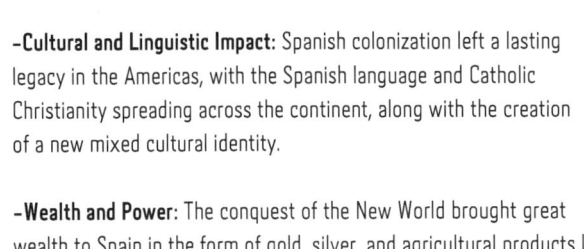

- **Cultural and Linguistic Impact:** Spanish colonization left a lasting legacy in the Americas, with the Spanish language and Catholic Christianity spreading across the continent, along with the creation of a new mixed cultural identity.

- **Wealth and Power:** The conquest of the New World brought great wealth to Spain in the form of gold, silver, and agricultural products like cocoa and tobacco, making the country one of the leading European powers in the 16th century.

49
Ancient History of Spain

1. Prehistory:
-**Period:** From the arrival of the first humans on the Iberian Peninsula, approximately 1.2 million years ago, until the arrival of Phoenician and Greek colonizers around the 8th century BCE.
-**Cultural Influence:** During prehistory, the Iberian populations developed a rich and diverse culture, as evidenced by cave paintings, tools, and megalithic structures. These cultures laid the foundations for subsequent societies on the peninsula.

2. Celts:
-**Period:** They settled on the Iberian Peninsula around the 8th century BCE.
-**Cultural Influence:** The Celts brought their own culture, including their language, religious beliefs, and metallurgical technology.
Their influence blended with preexisting cultures, contributing to the region's cultural diversity.

3. Iberians:
-**Period:** From the second millennium BCE until the Roman conquest in the 2nd century BCE.
-**Cultural Influence:** The Iberians developed an advanced culture, especially in agriculture, metallurgy, and urbanization.
Their art, architecture, and writing system left a lasting mark on the Iberian Peninsula.

4. Phoenician and Greek Colonization:
-**Period:** The Phoenicians established colonies on the southern coast starting in the 9th century BCE, followed by the Greeks on the eastern coast from the 7th century BCE.
-**Cultural Influence:** The Phoenicians and Greeks introduced writing, new trade techniques, and urbanization to the Iberian Peninsula. They also exchanged cultural and technological ideas with the local populations, further enriching the region's cultural diversity.

5. Carthaginians:

-Period: Carthage established its dominance on the Iberian Peninsula from the 3rd century BCE until the Second Punic War in the 2nd century BCE.

-Cultural Influence: The Carthaginians left their mark on the Iberian Peninsula through the founding of cities like Carthago Nova (Cartagena) and the establishment of trade routes. Their cultural legacy mixed with other Mediterranean cultures, contributing to the region's cultural diversity.

6. Roman History:

-Period: The Roman conquest of the Iberian Peninsula began in the 3rd century BCE and lasted until the fall of the Roman Empire in the 5th century CE.

-Cultural Influence: The Roman influence in Spain was profound and lasting. They introduced the Latin language, Roman law, architecture, engineering, and promoted the urbanization and Romanization of the local population. Many Spanish cities, such as Mérida (Emerita Augusta) and Tarragona (Tarraco), preserve significant Roman archaeological remains that testify to their influence.

Moreover, Christianity spread during this period, leaving an indelible mark on Spanish culture.

50

Spain is known for being one of the largest producers of olives and olive oil in the world.

1. Global Production: Spain is the largest producer of olives and olive oil in the world, accounting for a significant percentage of the total global production. Approximately 50% of the world's olive oil comes from Spain.

2. Main Regions:
- **Andalusia:** It is the leading olive oil-producing region in Spain, particularly the province of Jaén, which is considered the world capital of olive oil.
- **Extremadura:** It is also an important producing region, along with other regions like Castilla-La Mancha and Catalonia.

3. Olive Varieties:
- **Picual:** It is the most cultivated variety in Spain and the world. Its oil has a strong flavor and is rich in antioxidants.
- **Arbequina:** Produced mainly in Catalonia and Aragon, its oil is mild and fruity.
- **Hojiblanca:** Originating from Andalusia, it produces a mild oil with a hint of bitterness.

4. Production and Export:
- **Table Olives:** Spain is also a leader in table olive production, which are consumed directly.
- **Olive Oil:** Extra virgin olive oil is the star product. It is exported to many countries and is a staple ingredient of the Mediterranean diet.

5. History and Tradition: Olive cultivation in Spain has a long history, dating back to the times of the Phoenicians, Greeks, and Romans. For centuries, olive oil has been an integral part of Spanish gastronomy and economy.

6. Denominations of Origin: Spanish olive oil has several protected designations of origin (PDO) that guarantee its quality and origin, such as Sierra de Cazorla Designation of Origin Olive Oil or Bajo Aragón Olive Oil.

7. Economic Impact: The production of olives and olive oil is crucial to the agricultural economy of many Spanish regions, generating employment and local development.

8. Uses and Benefits: Olive oil is valued for its health benefits due to its high antioxidant content and healthy fats. Additionally, it is used in cooking, cosmetics, and medicine.

51

Spain is a parliamentary and constitutional monarchy.

1. Government Structure:
-**King:** He is the head of state. Currently, the King of Spain is Felipe VI. The king plays a primarily ceremonial role but also has important functions, such as representing Spain abroad, sanctioning laws approved by Parliament, and dissolving Parliament to call new elections.

-**Prime Minister:** The head of government, equivalent to the prime minister in other parliamentary systems. The prime minister is the leader of the political party that obtains the majority in Parliament, and their election is subject to parliamentary approval.

2. Parliament:
-**Congress of Deputies:** It is the lower house, made up of deputies elected by popular vote every four years.

-**Senate:** It is the upper house, with senators representing the autonomous communities, also elected by popular vote.

3. Powers of the King:
-**Representation:** Represents the Spanish State abroad and in official public events.

-**Royal Assent:** Sanctions and promulgates laws approved by Parliament.

-**Calling Elections:** Can dissolve the Cortes Generales and call elections at the proposal of the prime minister.

-**Military Command:** He is the supreme commander of the Armed Forces.

4. Recent History:
The monarchy was restored in Spain after the death of dictator Francisco Franco in 1975, with Juan Carlos I as king.

Since then, Spain has maintained its parliamentary monarchy system, with reforms to increase transparency and accountability.

Although the king has some important formal functions, real power is concentrated in the prime minister and Parliament.

52

Spain and Its Distinguished Soccer Tradition.

1. History of Soccer in Spain:
Soccer was introduced to Spain in the late 19th century.
The Royal Spanish Football Federation (RFEF) was founded in 1909 and organizes the main national competitions.

2. La Liga:
La Liga, or LaLiga Santander, is the top tier of Spanish soccer. Real Madrid and FC Barcelona are the most successful clubs with the fiercest rivalry. Other notable clubs include Atlético de Madrid, Valencia CF, and Sevilla FC.

3. Prominent Clubs:
-Real Madrid: Founded in 1902, it has won multiple La Liga titles and UEFA Champions League trophies, being one of the most successful clubs worldwide.
-FC Barcelona: Founded in 1899, it is another of the most successful clubs in Spain and the world, with numerous La Liga and Champions League victories.
-Atlético de Madrid: Founded in 1903, it is the third most successful club in Spain, with multiple league titles and European trophies.

4. National Team:
The Spanish national team, known as "La Roja," has won several major titles:
-World Cup in 2010.
-European Championships in 1964, 2008, and 2012.

The golden generation of players, including Xavi Hernández, Iker Casillas, Sergio Ramos, Andrés Iniesta, and others, was key to international success.

5. Playing Style:
Spain is known for its possession-based playing style, known as "tiki-taka," which became famous during the heyday of its national team and FC Barcelona.

6. Cultural Impact:
Soccer has a significant cultural impact in Spain. Club rivalries, especially "El Clásico" between Real Madrid and Barcelona, capture the attention of not only the country but also millions of fans worldwide.

53

Spain is famous for its many medieval castles, many of which are found in the historic regions of Castilla y León and Castilla-La Mancha.

1. Main Regions:
-**Castilla y León:** It has a high density of medieval castles, as it was a strategic area during the Reconquista. Some of the most well-known are the Castle of Coca, the Alcázar of Segovia, and the Castle of Ponferrada.
-**Castilla-La Mancha:** Also known for its abundance of castles, many of which were built during the Reconquista. Notable examples include the Castle of Alarcón, the Castle of Belmonte, and the Castle of Consuegra.

2. History:
Castle construction in Spain began during the Middle Ages, primarily as defensive structures. During the Reconquista, castles became strategic points in the fight against the Moors. Later, many castles became residential palaces for the nobility.

3. Architecture:
The architecture of castles varies depending on their period of construction, but many include features like towers, battlements, walls, and moats. Architectural styles include Romanesque, Gothic, and Mudejar, among others.

4. Tourism:
Tourist routes have been developed around castles, attracting history enthusiasts and tourists. Many routes include guided tours, events, and historical reenactments that allow visitors to experience life in medieval times.

5. Notable Castles:
-**Alcázar of Segovia:** Known for its distinctive ship-like shape, it is one of Spain's most famous castles.
-**Castle of Almodóvar:** Located in Andalusia, this castle has been restored and is often used for filming.
-**Castle of Peñafiel:** Located in Valladolid, it is an impressive example of medieval military architecture.

54

The Royal Spanish Academy (RAE) is a cultural institution founded
in 1713 with the purpose of maintaining and promoting
the proper use of the Spanish language.

1. History and Founders:
It was founded in 1713 at the initiative of Juan Manuel Fernández Pacheco, the 8th Marquis of Villena, with the purpose of establishing an authority to regulate the use of the Spanish language. The RAE was officially established in 1714 through a royal decree issued by King Philip V.

2. Purposes and Functions:
- **Language Regulation:** The RAE's primary objective is to ensure the purity, elegance, and splendor of the Spanish language. This includes the creation and revision of grammar and spelling rules.
- **Dictionary Creation:** The Diccionario de la lengua española, known as the DRAE, is its most recognized work. It also produces the Diccionario panhispánico de dudas and the Diccionario de americanismos.
- **Spelling Standards:** It publishes spelling and grammatical standards to unify language use in Spanish-speaking countries.
- **Associated Academies:** It works closely with other Spanish language academies in different Spanish-speaking countries through the Association of Spanish Language Academies (ASALE).

3. Publications:
- **Grammar:** The Nueva gramática de la lengua española is one of the most comprehensive works on the language's grammar.
- **Spelling:** The Ortografía de la lengua española sets forth the current spelling rules.
- **Dictionary:** The DRAE is its best-known dictionary and is used as the primary reference for the proper usage of words and definitions.

4. Evolution and Modernization:
The RAE has evolved over time, incorporating changes to the language according to modern trends. It has integrated digital technologies to offer online versions of its works and improve access to knowledge about the language.

5. Headquarters and Organization:
The RAE is headquartered in Madrid, Spain. The institution consists of academicians, also known as "full academicians," who are experts in the language and literature.

55

Spain is home to numerous megalithic monuments, prehistoric structures made of large stone blocks, which stand as evidence of the ingenuity and architecture of the earliest human civilizations.

1. Dolmen of Menga:
Located in Antequera, Málaga, the Dolmen of Menga is one of the largest megalithic monuments in Europe. It dates to the Neolithic or Copper Age, approximately between 3750 and 3650 BCE. It is made up of enormous stone slabs, some weighing over 180 tons. Its design is unusual because, instead of facing east like most dolmens, it is aligned to the north, towards a mountain known as La Peña de los Enamorados.

2. Other Megalithic Monuments in Spain:
- **Dolmen of Viera:** Also in Antequera, this dolmen is more aligned with typical Neolithic orientations, facing sunrise.
- **Tholos of El Romeral:** Near Antequera, this is a corridor tomb with a false dome, different from the dolmens of Menga and Viera.
- **Dolmen of Soto:** Located in Huelva, this is another example of a prehistoric funerary monument, with a long corridor and a rectangular chamber.

3. Function and Importance:
Megalithic monuments were generally used as burial sites, suggesting that they had ritual and religious significance. They may also have served as territorial landmarks to mark settlement boundaries.

4. World Heritage Site:
The Antequera Dolmens Site, which includes the dolmens of Menga, Viera, and El Romeral, was declared a UNESCO World Heritage Site in 2016.

5. Studies and Research:
Megalithic monuments are the subject of archaeological studies to better understand the prehistoric cultures that built them. They reveal information about the beliefs, social organization, and technical knowledge of ancient communities.

6. Tourism and Conservation:
Many megalithic monuments are open to the public, allowing visitors to explore their history and architecture. Conservation measures are taken to protect these sites from natural erosion and human impact.

56

The Day of the Three Kings, celebrated on January 6th, is one of the most important holidays in Spain, especially for children.

1. Origin and Significance:
-**History:** The holiday is based on the biblical story of the three Wise Men (Melchior, Gaspar, and Balthazar), who traveled from the East following a star to bring gifts to baby Jesus.
-**Religion:** It is a Christian holiday that marks the end of Christmas and celebrates the Epiphany, the moment when Jesus was revealed to the world as the Son of God.

2. Celebrations:
-**Parades:** On the eve of King's Day, January 5th, many Spanish cities hold parades, with actors dressed as the Wise Men and their companions distributing sweets to children.
-**Gifts:** On the morning of January 6th, children wake up to open the gifts that the Three Kings have left. It is similar to the Santa Claus tradition in other countries, but many Spanish children consider this day more important than Christmas.
-**Roscón de Reyes:** It is a tradition to share this ring-shaped sweet bread, decorated with candied fruit and with a surprise hidden inside. Whoever finds it is supposed to be "king" for the day.

3. Traditions:
-**Shoes and Straw:** The night before, children leave their shoes and sometimes straw or hay for the Three Kings' camels, expecting to find gifts in their place in the morning.
-**Letters:** Children write letters to the Three Kings, asking for the gifts they wish to receive.

4. Cultural Impact:
-**Events:** In many cities and towns, King's Day is a major celebration with community events, performances, and shows for all ages.
-**Economy:** It is a period of high commercial activity, as many families buy gifts for their loved ones.

5. Regional Variants:
-**Latin America:** King's Day is also celebrated in other Spanish-speaking countries, though customs may vary slightly.
-**Catalonia:** It is called "La Cavalcada de Reis" and has its own traditions, such as giving coal to children who have not behaved well.

The Day of the Three Kings remains a significant holiday in Spanish culture, especially for families and children.

57

Hispanic Day, celebrated on October 12th, has different meanings and celebrations across the Spanish-speaking world.

-Origin and History:
The date is traditionally associated with October 12, 1492, when Christopher Columbus arrived in what is now the American continent. It was established in Spain in 1918 under the name "Fiesta de la Raza" and later renamed "Hispanic Day" in 1958.

-Significance and Celebrations in Spain:
In Spain, Hispanic Day is a national holiday and is celebrated as the "National Day of Spain." Military parades and other official events take place, highlighting the unity of the country and its relationship with Spanish-speaking communities worldwide.

-Significance in Latin America:
In some Latin American countries, the date is celebrated as "Day of the Race" and focuses on cultural and ethnic diversity. Other countries, such as Chile and Peru, celebrate it as "Day of the Encounter of Two Worlds" or "Day of Indigenous Resistance," acknowledging the impact of the encounter between cultures.

-Other Names and Celebrations:
In the United States, October 12th is known as "Columbus Day" in commemoration of Christopher Columbus. Some states have changed the name to "Indigenous Peoples Day" to honor the contributions of native cultures.

In summary, Hispanic Day is celebrated in various ways depending on each country's historical and cultural context, but in general, it symbolizes the encounter between European and indigenous cultures, as well as the shared legacy of the Spanish language and culture.

58

Spain is known for its cultural richness, and an important part of that culture is the variety of traditional dances that vary by region.

-Flamenco: Originating from Andalusia, it is characterized by its emotional intensity and its combination of singing, guitar playing, and dancing. It has subgenres like fandango, soleá, and sevillana.

-Jota: Popular in Aragon, Navarre, and other regions. It is characterized by a fast rhythm and vigorous steps. It is often accompanied by castanets.

-Sardana: Originating from Catalonia, it is danced in a circle with participants holding hands. The music is usually played by a cobla (instrumental band).

-Muñeira: Traditional in Galicia and Asturias. Accompanied by bagpipes and tambourines, it has a fast rhythm and light steps.

-Sevillanas: Popular in Andalusia, they are danced in pairs and have a defined choreographic structure. They are performed at fairs and celebrations, especially during the April Fair in Seville.

-Fandango: An old style that is danced in many regions, but especially in Andalusia and Castilla-La Mancha. It has a fast rhythm and complex steps.

-Pasodoble: Inspired by the rhythm of a military march, it is often associated with the bullfighting environment.

-Zambra: Related to flamenco but with Moorish roots, it is traditionally danced at gypsy weddings in Granada.

These are just a few examples, as each region of Spain has its own repertoire of traditional dances that reflect the history and cultural influences of its area.

59

The Night of San Juan, which takes place on June 23rd and lasts until the early hours of June 24th, is one of the most popular celebrations in many regions.

It is a night that combines pagan and religious traditions and is linked to the summer solstice.

1. Origin and Meaning: It has roots in ancient pagan rituals related to the summer solstice, symbolizing the arrival of summer and the power of the sun. With Christianization, the festival became associated with the birth of Saint John the Baptist, celebrated on June 24th.

2. Bonfires: Bonfires are an essential element of the celebration. They symbolize purification and renewal. Traditionally, people jump over the bonfires to get rid of the old and start a new stage.

3. Beaches and Water Rituals: In coastal regions, the celebration includes rituals on the beaches. Many people bathe in the sea at midnight to purify themselves, and it is also common to jump over the waves.

4. Superstitions and Rituals: The Night of San Juan is full of superstitions and rituals to attract good luck. Some people write their wishes on paper and burn them in the bonfire, while others collect flowers and plants to keep throughout the year.

5. Celebrations in Different Regions:
-**Alicante:** The Bonfires of San Juan festival is especially well-known, with parades, music, and fireworks.
-**Galicia:** Bonfires and traditional foods like grilled sardines are typical.
-**Catalonia:** The beaches are filled with people enjoying bonfires and fireworks.
-**Menorca:** The San Juan festival in Ciutadella is very popular, with equestrian traditions.

6. Music and Dancing: Music and dancing are an essential part of the celebrations, with concerts and parties in many regions.

7. Gastronomy: The festivities also include typical dishes like grilled sardines and cocas (traditional cakes), which vary by region.

60

The Spanish Inquisition was an institution founded in 1478 during the reign of the Catholic Monarchs, Isabella I of Castile and Ferdinand II of Aragon.

Its main objective was to maintain Catholic orthodoxy in their kingdoms and to combat heresy.

-Foundation and Context: The Catholic Monarchs received permission from Pope Sixtus IV to establish an ecclesiastical court to maintain the purity of the Catholic faith. The Inquisition arose at a time when religious unity was considered essential for political and social stability.

-Functions and Purposes: Its primary purpose was to identify and judge heresies, but it also prosecuted blasphemy, Judaism, Islam, and any other doctrine that threatened Catholic orthodoxy. It particularly focused on the conversos, Jews converted to Christianity suspected of secretly practicing Judaism, and later on the Moriscos.

-Methods and Courts: The procedures were characterized by interrogations and torture to obtain confessions. Penalties ranged from fines and confiscation of property to death by burning, known as an auto-da-fé.

-Scope and Power: The Inquisition had a centralized structure, with courts in different regions. It had significant political and social power, influencing state politics and everyday life.

-Impact on Society: The Inquisition created a climate of fear and repression, limiting religious freedom and promoting uniformity. It had a negative impact on Jewish and Muslim communities, leading to forced conversions, persecution, and expulsions.

-Decline and Abolition: The Inquisition began to lose its power in the 18th century with Enlightenment reforms. It was finally officially abolished in 1834 during the reign of Isabella II.

-Legacy and Historical Perspective: The Spanish Inquisition left a legacy of religious intolerance and persecution. It is often used as a symbol of religious intolerance and religious authoritarianism in history.

61

The Middle Ages in Spain, approximately from the 5th to the 15th century, was a time of significant change, marked by the coexistence and conflict between Christians, Muslims, and Jews.

-**Visigothic Period (5th-8th centuries):** After the fall of the Roman Empire, the Visigoths established a kingdom on the Iberian Peninsula with Toledo as its capital. During this period, Christianity consolidated, and laws were codified, such as the Liber Iudiciorum.

-**Al-Andalus and the Caliphate of Córdoba (711-1031):** The Muslim invasion in 711 led to the creation of Al-Andalus. At its peak, the Caliphate of Córdoba was a cultural, scientific, and economic center known for its relative tolerance towards other religions.

-**Christian Kingdoms and the Reconquista (8th-15th centuries):** Northern Spain was the refuge of Christian kingdoms that began the Reconquista. The reconquest process lasted several centuries, with milestones such as the capture of Toledo in 1085 and the fall of Granada in 1492.

-**Cultural Coexistence and Conflict:** During periods of stability, there was relatively peaceful coexistence, known as "convivencia," between Muslims, Christians, and Jews. Learning centers were established, such as Toledo, where scientific and philosophical works were translated from Arabic and Greek into Latin.

-**Jews in Medieval Spain:** The Jews played a prominent role in the economy, administration, and medicine. Despite periods of tolerance, they also faced persecution, especially in the 14th century, culminating in their expulsion in 1492.

-**The Inquisition and the Expulsion of Muslims and Jews:** After the Reconquista, the Inquisition and royal decrees enforced forced conversions and the expulsion of Jews (1492) and Muslims (Moriscos, 1609-1614).

62

Laurel forests, also known as laurifolia or "laurel forests," are a type of subtropical forest that in Europe today can only be found in the Canary Islands and the island of Madeira.

These forests are a remnant of the vegetation that covered much of Europe during the Tertiary period, before the climatic changes of the Quaternary period.

-Vegetation: These forests are characterized by dense foliage and evergreen trees with large, thick leaves, similar to laurel, such as the Canary laurel (Laurus novocanariensis), til (Ocotea foetens), and viñátigo (Persea indica).
The undergrowth usually consists of ferns, mosses, and lichens that thrive in the humid and shaded environment.

-Climate and Location: They are typical of humid climates, with mild temperatures and constant rainfall, creating an environment similar to that of a subtropical rainforest. They are found in elevated and humid areas of the islands, between 500 and 1,500 meters above sea level.

-Canary Islands: The laurel forest is mainly found on the island of La Gomera, in Garajonay National Park (a UNESCO World Heritage Site). There are also laurel forests in Tenerife, especially in the Anaga Rural Park, and on other islands such as La Palma and El Hierro.

-Ecological Importance: They are a refuge for numerous endemic plant and animal species, many of them endangered. They play a crucial role in regulating water and preventing soil erosion.

-**Conservation:** Laurel forests have suffered significant reduction since the arrival of humans due to deforestation for agriculture and livestock farming. They are now protected in national parks and reserves, where conservation and reforestation efforts are carried out.

-**Cultural:** These forests have great cultural importance and are reflected in the history and mythology of the islands. They are popular destinations for sustainable tourism, with hiking trails that allow visitors to experience their biodiversity. One of the myths associated with the laurel forests is that of the nymphs and nature spirits that inhabit them.
These mystical creatures are believed to protect the forests and everything within them. It is said that at night, when moonlight filters through the leaves, it is possible to see these nymphs dancing among the trees while the nature spirits silently watch over them. Another legend suggests that at the heart of the laurel forests lies a magical place where time stands still and mortals can come into contact with the divine.
This place, often described as a clearing in the middle of the forest, is sought after by those seeking wisdom and healing. There are also stories of fantastic creatures that inhabit these forests, such as fairies, goblins, and elves.
These magical beings are said to be the guardians of the forests' flora and fauna, and those who venture into them must show respect and reverence toward them if they wish to return safely.

63

The Cave of Altamira, located near Santillana del Mar in Cantabria, Spain, is one of the world's most important archaeological sites.

Its cave paintings represent one of the most sophisticated expressions of Paleolithic art.

-Discovery: It was discovered in 1868 by the hunter Modesto Cubillas, but the importance of its contents was recognized in 1879 by Marcelino Sanz de Sautuola, a nobleman with an interest in archaeology.

-Cave Art: The cave is primarily known for its polychrome paintings of bison, horses, deer, and other animals. These paintings date from the Upper Paleolithic, approximately 36,000 to 13,000 years ago.
They are distinguished by their sophisticated technique, which includes the use of natural contours of the cave to add volume to the figures and the use of charcoal and iron oxide pigments.

-Structure of the Cave: The cave is 270 meters long and contains several galleries and chambers, the most famous being the Hall of Polychromes. In addition to the paintings, it contains engravings and portable art, providing a broader view of Paleolithic art.

-Study and Research: Initially, its authenticity was questioned, but subsequent research confirmed its genuineness.
Recent studies have demonstrated Altamira's key role in the development of European prehistoric art.

-Conservation and World Heritage: The massive influx of tourists led to the deterioration of the paintings, prompting the creation of a replica known as the Neocave, to allow study and observation without damaging the original site. In 1985, the Cave of Altamira was declared a UNESCO World Heritage Site.

-Cultural Importance: Altamira's paintings provide a unique insight into the artistic skills and lives of prehistoric humans. They represent a significant technical and artistic achievement for their time, with a realism and expression that astonished early scholars.

64

The Sima de la Cornisa is a cave located in Cantabria, Spain, known for being the deepest cave in the country, with a depth exceeding 1,500 meters.

This cave is a popular destination for speleologists and adventurers due to its impressive size and complexity.

Located in the Sierra de Arnero, near the village of La Hermida, Sima de la Cornisa is part of the cave system of the Ándara massif, one of the most important areas for speleology in Spain.

Access to this cave is difficult and requires specialized equipment and experience in speleology.

Exploring Sima de la Cornisa has been a constant challenge for speleologists, and numerous expeditions have been made to map and study this cave.

In addition to its depth, the cave features a complex network of galleries, narrow passages, and impressive rock formations.

Sima de la Cornisa is an outstanding example of the incredible underground world found in Spain and has significantly contributed to scientific knowledge of geology and speleology in the region.

However, due to its difficulty of access and the risks involved, it is important that those who wish to explore it be well-prepared and have the proper equipment.

65

Spain has a diversified economy with several major economic activities that are spread across different regions of the country.

1. Tourism:
-**Predominant Areas:** Coastal regions such as Catalonia, the Balearic Islands, the Canary Islands, the Costa del Sol in Andalusia, and the Costa Blanca in the Valencian Community.
-**Employment:** Tourism is a major source of employment in Spain, with around 12% of the total workforce employed in tourism-related sectors, which equals approximately 2.5 million people.

2. Agriculture:
-**Predominant Areas:** Andalusia, Valencia, Murcia, Castilla-La Mancha, and Catalonia are some of the most important regions for agriculture.
-**Employment:** Agriculture employs approximately 4% of the active population in Spain, which equates to around 800,000 people.

3. Industry:
-**Predominant Areas:** Catalonia, the Basque Country, Madrid, Valencia, and Andalusia are some of the most important industrial regions.
-**Employment:** The manufacturing industry employs around 14% of the active population in Spain, which equals approximately 2.9 million people.

4. Financial and Technological Services:
-**Predominant Areas:** Madrid is the country's main financial and technological hub, although Barcelona and other major cities also have a significant presence in these areas.
-**Employment:** The financial and technological services sector employs a significant portion of the active population in Spain, although no specific figure is available.

66

The island of Mallorca, located in the Mediterranean Sea and part of the Balearic Islands archipelago in Spain, is famous for hosting the largest network of underwater caves in Europe.

These underwater caves are a natural treasure and a world-renowned diving destination due to their stunning beauty and rich marine biodiversity.

The formation of these underwater caves is the result of geological processes that took place over millions of years. Through periods of sea level rise and fall, as well as the action of water erosion, a series of underwater cavities and passages were formed, creating this network of caves.

Mallorca has over 200 known underwater caves, although it is estimated that many more may still be undiscovered.

These caves vary in size, complexity, and geological features, creating a diverse and fascinating underwater environment for explorers and divers.

Among the most notable underwater caves in Mallorca is the Cova del Pas de Vallgornera, one of the largest in the world, with more than 7 kilometers of passageways and numerous impressive galleries and chambers.

Other notable underwater caves include Cova des Coloms, Cova des Pont, and Cova de sa Campana, each with its own charm and unique features.

Exploring these underwater caves offers divers the opportunity to discover incredible underwater landscapes, spectacular rock formations, and an astonishing variety of marine life, including fish, crustaceans, corals, and sponges.

However, it's important to highlight that exploring underwater caves carries certain risks and requires an appropriate level of experience, diving skills, and specialized equipment.

Many of these caves have narrow passages, unpredictable currents, and limited visibility conditions, making them suitable only for divers with proper training and preparation.

67

**The Salto del Nervión, located in the Basque Country,
is known as the tallest waterfall in Spain in terms of height.**

This impressive waterfall is situated in the Gorbea Natural Park, in the province of Álava, and is one of the most prominent natural wonders of the region.

The exact height of the Salto del Nervión varies according to sources, but it is estimated to be over 200 meters tall, making it one of the highest waterfalls on the Iberian Peninsula.

However, it's important to note that the waterfall does not flow consistently throughout the year, as its flow depends on precipitation and snowmelt in the region.

The Salto del Nervión is formed by the Nervión River, which runs through the Gorbea Natural Park and abruptly drops from a cliff in the mountains into the valley.

This natural spectacle is especially impressive after periods of heavy rain or during the snowmelt season, when the water flow is more abundant and the waterfall reaches its maximum splendor.

The area surrounding the Salto del Nervión is also remarkable for its scenic beauty, with spectacular mountain landscapes, lush forests, and green meadows that make it a popular destination for hikers and nature lovers.

Additionally, the area offers various hiking trails that allow visitors to enjoy panoramic views of the valley and the waterfall from different perspectives.

The Salto del Nervión is not only a natural point of interest but also a cultural and historical symbol in the Basque Country.

It has inspired numerous legends and folk tales over the centuries, and its majesty continues to captivate those who have the opportunity to witness it in person.

68

The Picos de Europa National Park is one of the most impressive and emblematic natural areas in Spain.

It is located in the autonomous communities of Asturias, Cantabria, and Castilla y León, in northern Spain.

This park is famous for its stunning mountainous landscape, deep gorges, impressive peaks, and rich biodiversity.

-Size and Location: As you mentioned, the Picos de Europa National Park is the largest protected area in Spain, with an area exceeding 60,000 hectares. It spans three provinces: Asturias, Cantabria, and León, covering part of the Cantabrian Mountains.

-Mountain Landscape: The Picos de Europa are known for their spectacular mountainous landscape, which includes rugged peaks, deep valleys, gorges, and a series of impressive rock formations. Among its most notable peaks are Naranjo de Bulnes (also known as Picu Urriellu), Torre Cerredo, and Pico Tesorero.

-Flora and Fauna: The park harbors exceptional biological diversity, with a wide variety of habitats ranging from alpine meadows to oak and beech forests. It is home to numerous species of flora and fauna, including the Cantabrian brown bear, the capercaillie, the bearded vulture, and a wide variety of birds of prey, mammals, reptiles, and amphibians.

-Outdoor Activities: The Picos de Europa National Park offers a wide range of outdoor activities for visitors, including hiking, climbing, mountaineering, mountain biking, caving, birdwatching, and water sports on the area's rivers and lakes.

-Culture and Traditions: In addition to its natural value, the park also has a rich cultural heritage and deep-rooted traditions in the local communities that surround it. These communities have developed a unique way of life in harmony with the natural environment and maintain a rich gastronomic and artisanal tradition.

69

In Spain, there are several historical relics and legendary objects that have captured the popular imagination over the centuries.

-The Holy Grail: The Holy Grail is said to be the chalice used by Jesus Christ at the Last Supper. The legend of the Holy Grail has been the subject of numerous stories, myths, and literary works throughout history. In Spain, Valencia Cathedral claims to hold the authentic Holy Grail in its collection.

-The Shroud of Turin: Although currently located in Turin, Italy, the Shroud of Turin is one of the most important and controversial Christian relics in the world. It is said to be the cloth that wrapped the body of Jesus Christ after his crucifixion. The shroud has been the subject of intense scientific research and debate.

-The Spear of Destiny: Also known as the Holy Lance, this spear is said to have been used by the Roman centurion Longinus to pierce the side of Jesus Christ during the crucifixion. The spear has been the subject of numerous legends and myths throughout history. According to tradition, the spear is housed in Valencia Cathedral.

-The Cross of Caravaca: This cross is a revered religious symbol in the town of Caravaca de la Cruz, in the Region of Murcia. Legend has it that the cross was miraculously brought by two angels and has healing and protective powers.

-The Brotherhood of the Vera Cruz of Oviedo: This religious brotherhood is located in the city of Oviedo, in Asturias, and guards several relics related to the Passion of Christ, including fragments of the True Cross, the Holy Lance, and the Sudarium of Oviedo, which is said to be the cloth that covered the face of Jesus Christ after his death.

-The Cathedral of Santiago de Compostela and the Holy Shroud: The Cathedral of Santiago de Compostela, in Galicia, is one of the most important Christian pilgrimage destinations in the world. It houses the supposed tomb of the Apostle James. Additionally, the cathedral is said to house the Holy Shroud, which was used to wrap the body of James after his martyrdom.

-The Virgin of the Pillar: The Virgin of the Pillar is a Marian devotion venerated in Zaragoza, in the Basilica of Our Lady of the Pillar. According to Catholic tradition, the Virgin Mary appeared to the Apostle James in Zaragoza and gave him a pillar as a symbol of her protection. The basilica houses a marble column believed to be the original pillar.

-The Chalice of Doña Urraca: This chalice, located in the Cathedral of San Salvador de Oviedo, is believed to be the chalice used by Queen Doña Urraca, daughter of Ferdinand I of León, during the celebration of the Eucharist. Although its authenticity is disputed, the chalice is considered an important historical relic in Spain.

-The Bell Gable of San Martín de Tours: The Church of San Martín de Tours, in the town of Frómista, in the province of Palencia, houses a bell gable believed to be of Visigothic origin. This bell gable is one of the few surviving Visigothic architectural relics in Spain and is a remarkable example of the art and architecture of that era.

-The Holy Ark of the Oviedo Cathedral: This chest, located in the Holy Chamber of the Cathedral of Oviedo, is venerated as an important Christian relic. It is said to contain several sacred objects, including a fragment of the True Cross, the Holy Shroud, and a nail from the crucifixion of Christ.

70

The Neanderthals in Spain, like in other parts of Europe, were a species of hominid that inhabited the region approximately between 400,000 and 40,000 years ago, during the Middle and Upper Paleolithic.

They had distinctive physical characteristics, such as robust bodies and adaptations to cold climates, with elongated and prominent skulls, large jaws, and wide noses.

Their culture included stone tools, cave art, and possibly burial practices.

Neanderthals in Spain have been primarily found at archaeological sites such as Sima de los Huesos in the Sierra de Atapuerca, Abric Romani in Catalonia, Cueva del Sidrón in Asturias, and El Salt in Alicante, among others.

These sites have provided valuable information about the life and behavior of Neanderthals on the Iberian Peninsula.

Regarding genetic mixing with the modern population, genetic studies have shown that Neanderthals contributed genetic material to modern humans outside of Africa.

It is estimated that between 1% and 2% of the DNA of modern non-African populations comes from Neanderthals, suggesting that there were interactions and possibly mating between Neanderthals and modern humans in the past.

This percentage may vary slightly depending on the region and ethnic group.

71

Spain has an extensive network of toll highways, making it one of the countries with the highest number of kilometers of these roads in Europe.

-Length of the Toll Highway Network: The network of toll highways in Spain exceeds 3,000 kilometers in length.
These toll highways extend throughout the country, connecting important regions and cities.

-National and International Connections: Toll highways in Spain are vital for the country's connectivity, linking major cities and regions, facilitating the transport of people and goods. Additionally, some toll highways also connect Spain with neighboring countries, such as France and Portugal, forming part of important European transport corridors.

-Management and Operation: Toll highways in Spain are managed and operated by various companies, both public and private.
Some of these companies hold concessions for specific highway sections, while others operate nationwide. Users of these highways must pay a toll to use them, which varies depending on the distance traveled and the type of vehicle.

-Quality and Services: Toll highways in Spain usually offer high standards of quality and safety, with wide lanes, clear signage, and additional services such as rest areas, gas stations, and service areas for emergency vehicles. Many of these highways are equipped with electronic toll systems (tele-toll) that streamline payments and reduce waiting times at toll booths.

-Usage and Popularity: Despite the tolls, these highways remain a popular choice for many drivers, especially those seeking faster and more comfortable routes, with less traffic and better road conditions. However, there are also free alternatives, such as national roads and dual carriageways, used by those who prefer to avoid paying tolls.

72

Spain's history is full of myths and legends related to witches and sorcerers.

-The Witch of Guadarrama: In the Sierra de Guadarrama, near Madrid, there's a legend of a witch who lived deep in the forest.
According to the story, this witch had the power to transform into different creatures to stalk travelers who ventured through the forest at night. It was said she had made a pact with the devil and that her evil laughter could be heard on full moon nights. Many locals avoided entering the forest for fear of encountering this feared witch.

-The Witch Burnings of Zugarramurdi: In the 17th century, in the town of Zugarramurdi in the Basque Country, one of the darkest episodes related to the witch hunt in Spain took place. A trial known as the Auto-da-Fé of Logroño was held in 1610, where dozens of people, mostly women, were accused of witchcraft and heresy. Many of them were burned at the stake after confessing under torture. This event has been etched into the region's collective memory and is remembered as a moment of intolerance and violence toward those considered practitioners of witchcraft.

-The Witch of Bargota: In the town of Bargota in Navarre, there is a story about a woman known as the "Witch of Bargota." According to legend, this woman had supernatural powers and practiced witchcraft in secret. It was said that she could cast curses and spells on those who crossed her path. The story of the Witch of Bargota has been passed down through generations in the town, and her figure still inspires fear among some locals.

-The Legend of the Enchanted Woman of Trasmoz: Trasmoz, a small town in Aragon, is known for its history of witchcraft and magic.
According to legend, a woman named La Encantada de Trasmoz practiced witchcraft in the town's ancient fortress. It was said she had the power to cast spells and curses on those who dared to challenge her. Legend has it that after her death, her spirit continues to roam the ruins of the fortress, casting her spells on unwary visitors. This story has contributed to Trasmoz's reputation as one of Spain's most haunted towns.

73

Spain has had its share of cases and sightings of phenomena related to what is considered ufology.

-**Manises Case (1979):** This case occurred on November 11, 1979, when a commercial aircraft of the TAE (Transports Aériens Intercontinentaux) company was approaching Manises Airport in Valencia. The crew reported the presence of a luminous object that appeared to follow the plane and emitted intense flashes. The pilot decided to perform evasive maneuvers and made an emergency landing. The Spanish Air Force sent fighter jets to investigate but found nothing. This case has been studied by researchers in ufology and aviation, generating numerous theories about its origin.

-**Puerto de Santa María Case (1989):** On the night of November 4, 1989, sightings of strange lights and unidentified objects were reported in the sky near the Rota Naval Base in Cádiz. Several people, including military personnel from the base, claimed to have seen bright lights and moving objects that could not be identified as conventional aircraft. This event attracted the attention of both national and international media and was the subject of speculation and analysis by paranormal researchers.

-**Vicalvaro Case (1994):** In this case, which occurred in 1994 in Madrid, several residents of Vicalvaro reported sightings of an unidentified flying object in the area. According to reports, the object was large and luminous and moved erratically in the night sky. This case stood out for the number of eyewitnesses and generated considerable interest in the local media.

-**San José de Valderas Case (2004):** On the night of May 11, 2004, several witnesses in Alcorcón, Madrid, reported seeing a luminous and silent object in the night sky. The object was described as large and bright and moved peculiarly before disappearing.
This sighting attracted the attention of the local media and was investigated by UFO enthusiasts.

74

Spain has been an important location for the discovery of dinosaur fossils, and different types of these fascinating reptiles have been found.

1. Iguanodon bernissartensis:
-**Characteristics**: This herbivorous dinosaur was known for its parrot-like beak and leaf-shaped teeth. It walked both on two and four legs.
-**Location Found**: Iguanodon remains have been found in various places in Spain, including the regions of Teruel and Cuenca.
-**Physical Description**: It had a robust body with short, strong forelimbs and longer hind limbs. It could measure around 10 meters long.
-**Era**: During the Cretaceous period, approximately 125-90 million years ago.

2. Ampelosaurus:
-**Characteristics**: This dinosaur was a herbivorous sauropod, characterized by its long neck and tail and massive body.
-**Location Found**: Ampelosaurus fossils have been found in the Catalonia region, in northeastern Spain.
-**Physical Description**: Ampelosaurus was estimated to be around 15 meters long and weighed several tons.
-**Era**: During the Cretaceous period, approximately 70-66 million years ago.

3. Turiasaurus riodevensis:
-**Characteristics**: This sauropod was one of the largest known dinosaurs, with a long neck and tail, and a massive body.
-**Location Found**: Its remains have been discovered in the province of Teruel, in the Aragon region.
-**Physical Description**: Turiasaurus was estimated to reach lengths of up to 30 meters and weigh around 40 tons.
-**Era**: Also during the Cretaceous period, approximately 145-140 million years ago.

4. Concavenator corcovatus:
-**Characteristics:** This theropod dinosaur was notable for a distinctive hump on its back, possibly for fat storage or courtship. It also had large claws on its forelimbs.
-**Location Found:** Its fossils were discovered in the province of Teruel, in the Aragon region.
-**Physical Description:** Concavenator was approximately 6 meters long and had an appearance similar to that of tyrannosaurs but smaller in size.
-**Era:** During the Cretaceous period, about 130 million years ago.

5. Losillasaurus giganteus:
-**Characteristics:** This dinosaur was a moderately-sized herbivorous sauropod, with a long neck and tail.
-**Location Found:** Fossils were discovered in the town of Losilla, in the province of Teruel.
-**Physical Description:** Losillasaurus was about 12 meters long and had a neck that helped it reach tall vegetation.
-**Era:** Also during the Cretaceous period, approximately 130 million years ago.

6. Proa valdearinnoensis:
-**Characteristics:** This small theropod dinosaur was similar in size and appearance to a velociraptor. It is believed to have been an agile hunter.
-**Location Found:** It was discovered in the town of El Castellar, in the province of Teruel.
-**Physical Description:** Proa was relatively small, at approximately 2 meters long.
-**Era:** During the Jurassic period, about 145 million years ago.

7. Megalosaurus bucklandii:
-**Characteristics:** This theropod dinosaur was one of the largest carnivores of its time. It had sharp teeth and powerful claws on its forelimbs.
-**Location Found:** Megalosaurus fossils have been found in various regions of Spain, including Catalonia and Teruel.
-**Physical Description:** Megalosaurus was estimated to reach a length of around 9 meters.
-**Era:** During the Jurassic period, approximately 166-140 million years ago.

75

Classic scams in Spain that involve deceptive tactics:

-**El Tocomocho**: The scammer approaches the victim and shows them a supposedly winning lottery ticket but claims they can't cash it due to some excuse (such as not having identification or being a foreigner). The scammer then proposes to sell the ticket for less than its value, apparently to get quick cash. The victim, thinking they can make a profit, buys the ticket but discovers it's fake when they try to cash it.

-**El Timo de la Estampita**: A scammer pretends to be a person with a mental disability, showing an envelope full of colored papers or newspaper clippings that look like banknotes. They pretend not to understand its value and offer the envelope to the victim for a much lower price. Sometimes, an accomplice acts as a middleman, urging the victim to buy the envelope, making them believe it's full of real money.

-**The Banknote Switch Scam**: The scammer asks for change for a high-value banknote (for example, a 100-euro bill). While the change is being counted, the scammer distracts the victim with some excuse to manipulate the money, like adding or subtracting bills, thereby keeping a larger amount or a counterfeit bill.

-**The Gasoline Scam**: Scammers pretend to be in a desperate situation, saying that their car has run out of gas and they need money to refuel. They often offer to return the money after going to an ATM or to their bank. However, after receiving the money, they disappear without a trace.

-**El Nazareno**: The scammers create a fictitious company that operates for a while to gain trust with suppliers. They make small orders initially and pay on time, but later, they make large orders on credit. Once they receive the products, they disappear with them without paying.

-**The Hotel Key Scam**: A scammer poses as a hotel employee and calls the victim's room, telling them that they need to confirm the credit card for a payment or reservation. Taking advantage of the victim's trust in the hotel, the scammer obtains the card information and uses it to make fraudulent charges.

76
Statistics about couples.

1. Marriages:
-Marriage Rate: In 2022, the marriage rate was 3.4 per 1,000 inhabitants, according to the National Institute of Statistics (INE). This shows a downward trend compared to previous decades.

-Average Age at Marriage: The average age at marriage has increased. In 2021, the average age for men was around 39, and for women, around 36.

2. Divorces:
-Divorce Rate: The divorce rate showed an increase until the mid-2000s and a subsequent stabilization. In 2021, there were approximately 85,000 divorces, according to the INE.

-Average Marriage Duration: The average duration of marriages before divorce is around 16 years.

3. Number of Children:
-Birth Rate: The birth rate in Spain has been declining. In 2022, the fertility rate was around 1.19 children per woman, one of the lowest rates in Europe.

-Average Age of Mothers: The average age for having a first child has increased over time, reaching 32 years.

4. Infidelities:
Statistics on infidelity are difficult to obtain accurately. Some studies suggest that between 20-30% of respondents have admitted to some form of infidelity.

77

**In Spain, there is a great variety of fauna
due to its geographical and climatic diversity.**

-**Iberian Lynx:** One of the most endangered felines in the world. It is mainly found in Andalusia (Doñana and Sierra de Andújar). There are about 1,100 individuals in the wild.

-**Spanish Imperial Eagle:** A bird of prey endemic to the Iberian Peninsula. It is located in regions like Castilla-La Mancha, Extremadura, and Andalusia. Its population is growing, with around 600 pairs.

-**Brown Bear:** Inhabits the mountains of northern Spain (Cantabrian Mountains and Pyrenees). Its population is estimated at around 350 individuals.

-**Spanish Ibex:** A species of wild goat found in many Spanish mountains, including the Sierra de Gredos, the Central System, and the mountains of Andalusia. Its population is abundant, with tens of thousands of specimens.

-**Cantabrian Capercaillie:** A subspecies of the capercaillie, endemic to the Cantabrian Mountains. It is critically endangered, with a population of around 300 individuals.

-**Mediterranean Monk Seal:** Although historically present on the Spanish Mediterranean coasts, it is now very rare, and its population is mainly concentrated in the eastern Mediterranean.

-**White Stork:** It is common throughout Spain, especially in the northern half. It is estimated that there are more than 30,000 breeding pairs in the country.

-**Bearded Vulture:** A scavenger bird that mainly inhabits the Pyrenees. Its population is estimated at around 150 breeding pairs.

-**Greater Mouse-eared Bat:** A common bat species in Europe, including Spain. Its exact numbers are unclear, but it is considered relatively common.

-**Comber:** A fish typical of the waters of the Mediterranean and eastern Atlantic. It is common on Spanish coasts, and although there are no exact data, it is an abundant species.

- **Natterjack Toad:** A common amphibian on the peninsula, especially in lowland areas and plains. Its population is stable.

- **Moorish Tortoise:** A species of terrestrial tortoise mainly found in southeastern Spain. Although it is endangered, it is estimated that several thousand individuals remain.

- **Wildcat:** A feline native to Europe that inhabits Spanish forests. Although difficult to spot, its population is stable.

- **Alpine Newt:** An amphibian that lives in the Pyrenees and other mountainous areas in the north. There are no precise data on its population.

- **Montpellier Snake:** One of the largest snakes in Europe, present in much of the Iberian Peninsula.

- **Iberian Wolf:** This predator is mainly found in northwestern Spain, in regions such as Castilla y León, Galicia, and Asturias. The estimated population is around 2,500 individuals.

- **Ocellated Lizard:** One of the largest lizards in Europe, inhabiting most of the Iberian Peninsula and southern France.

- **Roe Deer:** A small deer found in most wooded areas of Spain. Its population is numerous and expanding.

- **Griffon Vulture:** One of the largest scavenger birds in Europe, common in many mountainous areas of Spain. It is estimated that there are more than 25,000 breeding pairs in the country.

- **Snub-nosed Viper:** A venomous snake endemic to the Iberian Peninsula. It is common in many areas of Spain, although it is not aggressive and avoids human contact.

- **Marbled Newt:** An amphibian found in many humid regions of the peninsula, especially in the northern half.

- **Cabrera's Vole:** A small rodent endemic to the Iberian Peninsula that inhabits wet areas and grasslands.

- **Lesser Kestrel:** A small falcon that breeds in colonies and is found in southwestern Europe. Its population has declined, but several thousand pairs remain.

78

Spain has a variety of protected marine reserves along its extensive coastline.

-Cabo de Palos - Islas Hormigas Marine Reserve (Murcia):
This reserve is located in the Murcia region, in southeastern Spain. It is known for its marine diversity, including Posidonia meadows and species like groupers, croakers, and moray eels.

-Islas Columbretes Marine Reserve (Valencian Community):
Located off the coast of Castellón in the Valencian Community, this reserve protects a volcanic archipelago that is home to rich marine biodiversity, including species like Posidonia, coralline algae, and various species of fish.

-Isla de Tabarca Marine Reserve (Valencian Community):
This reserve is off the coast of Alicante and is known for its important ecological and scenic value. It is home to a variety of marine fauna, including fish, crustaceans, and mollusks.

-Isla de Alborán Marine Reserve (Andalusia):
Located in the Alboran Sea, between the Iberian Peninsula and North Africa, this reserve protects an area of great marine biodiversity, including Posidonia meadows, corals, and various species of cetaceans.

-La Graciosa Marine Reserve (Canary Islands):
This reserve is located on the island of La Graciosa, in the Canary archipelago. It protects a unique marine ecosystem, with crystal-clear waters and a great diversity of marine species, including sea turtles, cetaceans, and tropical fish.

-Cabo Tiñoso Marine Reserve (Murcia):
Located in the Murcia region, this reserve protects a rocky stretch of coastline with rich marine biodiversity, including corals, sponges, and various species of fish.

These are just a few of the most notable marine reserves in Spain, but there are many more distributed along its coastline that contribute to the conservation and protection of its valuable marine ecosystems.

79

**The shipwrecks found in Spain are remnants of vessels
that have wrecked or sunk in its waters throughout history.**

Spain, with its extensive coastline bathed by the Mediterranean Sea, the Atlantic Ocean, and the Cantabrian Sea, is home to a wide variety of shipwrecks dating from antiquity to the modern era.

-Number of Shipwrecks: It is estimated that there are hundreds, even thousands, of shipwrecks in Spanish waters due to its rich maritime history and the intense naval and commercial activity that has taken place in the region over the centuries.

-Types of Shipwrecks: The shipwrecks found in Spain can be of various types, including warships, merchant ships, fishing vessels, Roman and Phoenician ships, and other types of ancient and modern vessels.

-Examples of Shipwrecks in Spain:

1. The Galleon Nuestra Señora de las Mercedes: This is one of the most famous shipwrecks found in Spanish waters. It is a Spanish galleon that sank off the coast of Portugal in 1804. The wreck was discovered by treasure hunters in 2007 and later recovered by the Spanish government. It contained a valuable cargo of silver coins and other treasures.

2. The Wreck of the Frigate Nuestra Señora de las Mercedes: Another historically important vessel, the frigate Nuestra Señora de las Mercedes, sank near the coast of Portugal in 1804. It was one of the ships of the Spanish fleet carrying riches from South America to Spain. The remains of the wreck, including part of the cargo of gold and silver, were recovered by the Spanish government in 2012.

3. The Phoenician Ship Mazarrón II: This wreck is an example of a Phoenician ship found on the Mediterranean coast of Spain. It is a cargo ship dating from the 7th century BCE that was discovered in the waters near Mazarrón, in the Murcia region. It contained valuable commercial goods such as silver ingots, amphorae, and other artifacts.

4. The Bou Ferrer Shipwreck: This is one of the most important Roman shipwrecks found in Spain. It is a Roman merchant ship that wrecked in the 1st century CE near the coast of Villajoyosa, in the province of Alicante.
The wreck contained a large number of amphorae and other artifacts that provide valuable information about maritime trade in ancient Rome.

80

Spain is one of the leading producers of saffron in the world and is known for the high quality of its production.

-Producing Regions: Most of Spain's saffron production comes from specific regions that have suitable climatic and soil conditions for growing this spice. Some of the most important regions include La Mancha, in the province of Ciudad Real, Castilla y León, Aragón, and some areas of Andalusia.

-Climate and Soil: Saffron is a plant that prefers temperate climates and well-drained soils. The saffron-producing regions in Spain usually have cold winters and dry summers, which provide ideal conditions for cultivating this spice.

-Cultivation Method: Saffron is traditionally grown in small plots of land called "rosales." The bulbs of the saffron flower are planted in the fall, and the flowers bloom in the spring. The red stigmas of the flowers, which are the saffron threads, are picked by hand and then dried for use as a spice.

-Quality and Designation of Origin: The quality of Spanish saffron is highly regarded worldwide due to its distinctive flavor, aroma, and color. The Protected Designation of Origin (PDO) Azafrán de La Mancha is a certification that guarantees the quality and authenticity of saffron produced in the La Mancha region, which is one of the most recognized and valued.

-Uses and Applications: Saffron is used in cooking to add flavor, aroma, and color to various dishes, especially in Spanish cuisine, where it is used in paellas, soups, stews, and rice dishes. It is also used in traditional medicine and the cosmetics and perfume industry due to its antioxidant and anti-inflammatory properties.

In summary, Spain is the largest producer of saffron in the world, with more than 1 ton produced each year.

The quality and reputation of Spanish saffron make the country a leader in the production and export of this precious spice.

81

Spain is a notable destination for astronomical observation due to its clear skies, low light pollution, and the presence of numerous astronomical observatories distributed throughout the country.

-Variety of Observatories: Spain has a wide variety of astronomical observatories, ranging from small local facilities to internationally renowned scientific complexes. These observatories are dedicated to the study of space, astronomy, astrophysics, and related disciplines.

-Favorable Geographical Location: Spain's geography offers ideal conditions for astronomical observation, with numerous areas of dark skies and low light pollution in many parts of the country.
This makes Spain an attractive destination for professional and amateur astronomers, as well as tourists interested in astronomy.

-Scientific Institutions and Universities: Many of the astronomical observatories in Spain are associated with renowned scientific institutions and universities, such as the Canary Islands Institute of Astrophysics (IAC), the Center for Astrobiology (CAB), the National Astronomical Observatory (OAN), and various Spanish universities.

-Research and International Collaboration: Spain is actively involved in astronomical research at the international level and collaborates with other countries on scientific projects and programs.
Spanish observatories contribute to important discoveries and advances in astronomy and astrophysics.

-Astronomical Tourism: In addition to their scientific use, many astronomical observatories in Spain offer outreach programs and activities for the public, such as guided tours, workshops, talks, and astronomical observation sessions.
These activities attract tourists interested in astronomy and contribute to the development of astronomical tourism in the country.

Some notable examples of astronomical observatories in Spain include the Teide Observatory in Tenerife, the Calar Alto Observatory in Almería, the Sierra Nevada Observatory in Granada, and the Mallorca Astronomical Observatory, among others.

82

Spain has a great diversity of butterflies, with over 2,000 different species recorded in the country.

-Variety of Habitats: Spain has a wide range of habitats, from Mediterranean forests and mountains to wetlands, grasslands, and coasts. These diverse environments provide suitable conditions for a great diversity of butterflies, each adapted to its own ecological niche.

-Migratory Routes: Spain is part of the migratory routes of butterflies, especially on the Iberian Peninsula and the Canary Islands. During their seasonal migrations, many butterfly species pass through Spain in search of more favorable climatic conditions or suitable breeding sites.

-Endemic and Unique Species: Spain is home to numerous endemic butterfly species, meaning those found exclusively in specific geographic regions. There are also unique and rare species found in specific habitats that are of interest to entomologists and nature lovers.

-Observation and Study Areas: Spain offers numerous areas for the observation and study of butterflies, including natural parks, nature reserves, botanical gardens, and protected areas. These places provide opportunities for sighting, studying, and conserving butterflies and their habitats.

-Conservation and Protection: The conservation of butterflies and their habitats is important in Spain, and conservation programs and projects are carried out to protect endangered species and their natural habitats. This includes measures such as habitat restoration, protected area management, and public awareness of the importance of biodiversity.

Some of the most notable butterfly species in Spain include the Monarch Butterfly (Danaus plexippus), the Swallowtail (Papilio machaon), the Apollo (Parnassius apollo), the Spanish Moon Moth (Graellsia isabellae), and many more.

83

Coastal watchtowers, also known as lookout towers, watchtowers, or coastal defense towers, are historic structures built along the coasts for surveillance and defense against pirate and maritime enemy attacks.

-Purpose and Construction: Coastal watchtowers were primarily built during periods of conflict and piracy in Spain's history, including the Middle Ages, the Renaissance, and the time of the Barbary raids.
Their purpose was to detect and alert about potential enemy attacks from the sea, as well as to protect the coasts and coastal populations.

-Distribution and Location: Coastal watchtowers are distributed along the extensive Spanish coastline, from the Mediterranean Sea to the Atlantic Ocean and the Cantabrian Sea. They are found in strategic locations such as capes, promontories, cliffs, and harbor entrances, which offer a panoramic view of the sea and allow for rapid visual communication between nearby towers.

-Architecture and Design: Coastal watchtowers vary in size, shape, and architectural design, depending on the era and region in which they were built. Some are cylindrical towers, while others are square or rectangular. Many are built with local stone and have defensive features such as thick walls, narrow windows, and battlements.

-Notable Examples:

1. Torre de Guadalmesí (Cádiz): This tower is located in the province of Cádiz, in Andalusia, and is one of the oldest coastal watchtowers in Spain, dating from the 15th century. It was part of the coastal defensive system to protect against pirate attacks in the Strait of Gibraltar.
2. Tower of Hercules (A Coruña): Although technically not a coastal watchtower in the traditional sense, the Tower of Hercules is a Roman lighthouse located in A Coruña, Galicia. It is the oldest functioning lighthouse in the world and has served as a navigation landmark for centuries.
3. Ibiza Watchtowers: On the island of Ibiza in the Balearic Islands, several coastal watchtowers were built during the 16th and 17th centuries to protect against pirate and privateer attacks. These towers, such as the Torre de Ses Portes and the Torre des Carregador, are examples of defensive architecture in the region.

84

Spain is a popular destination for water park enthusiasts, boasting a wide variety of parks offering fun and entertainment for the whole family, with over 50 options.

-Siam Park - Tenerife: Located on the island of Tenerife, in the Canary Islands, Siam Park is one of the largest and most popular water parks in Europe. With a Thai theme, the park offers a wide variety of water slides, wave pools, lazy rivers, and relaxation areas. It stands out for its spectacular wave pool, considered the largest in the world.

-PortAventura Caribe Aquatic Park - Salou: Part of the PortAventura World complex, located in Salou on the Catalan coast, this themed water park has a Caribbean atmosphere and offers a wide variety of slides, pools, water play areas, and relaxation zones. It is one of the largest water parks in Spain and attracts visitors of all ages.

-Aqualandia - Benidorm: Located in Benidorm, on the Mediterranean coast, Aqualandia is one of the oldest water parks in Spain and remains one of the most popular. It offers a wide range of water attractions, including high-speed slides, wave pools, lazy rivers, children's play areas, and relaxation zones.

-Aquopolis - Costa Dorada: This water park is located in La Pineda, near Salou, on the Costa Dorada of Catalonia. It offers a variety of water attractions for the whole family, such as water slides, wave pools, children's play areas, and live aquatic shows. It also features relaxation zones and picnic areas.

-Aquashow Park - Albufeira: Although technically located in Portugal, near the city of Albufeira in the Algarve, Aquashow Park is very popular among Spanish visitors due to its proximity to the border.
This water park offers a wide range of water attractions, including water slides, wave pools, lazy rivers, and water play areas.

These are just a few examples of the numerous water parks that can be found in Spain, offering fun and entertainment for the whole family during the summer months.

Each park has its own charm and unique attractions, but they all share the goal of providing a refreshing and exciting experience for their visitors.

85

The Madrid Metro is the subway system of the capital and one of the largest metro networks in the world.

-History: It was inaugurated in 1919, making it one of the first metro networks in Europe. Line 1, which connected Cuatro Caminos with Sol, had only 8 stations and a length of 3.5 km.

-Expansion: Since its inauguration, the system has undergone significant expansion, particularly in the 1990s and 2000s. It now covers much of Madrid city and some nearby municipalities.

-Stations: The Madrid Metro has 13 lines and over 300 stations, with a total length of around 294 km. It is the third largest metro in Europe, after those of London and Moscow.

-Depth: The deepest station is Cuatro Caminos, about 45 meters deep. Several lines and stations are at different levels, with connections between them.

-Innovation: The metro has pioneered the implementation of new technologies, such as free Wi-Fi in its stations and the use of driverless trains on some lines.

-Architecture: Many stations have notable architectural designs, such as Chamartín station, which features murals, or the modern Chamartín station, with its minimalist design.

-Complementary Network: In addition to the main lines, the metro has complementary lines, such as the Metro Ligero and the special Ramal Ópera-Príncipe Pío line, which connect with less accessible areas.

-Services: The Madrid Metro offers additional services such as "Bibliometro," which allows passengers to borrow books at certain stations.

-Payment Systems: The payment system is highly digitized, allowing the use of transport cards, monthly passes, and electronic tickets.

-Accessibility: Although not all stations are accessible, significant efforts have been made to adapt many with elevators and ramps.

-Connections: The metro has strategic connections with Adolfo Suárez Madrid-Barajas Airport, train stations like Atocha and Chamartín, and other public transport services like buses and commuter trains.

-Art in the Metro: Some stations stand out for their art exhibitions and mosaics that reflect the history and culture of Madrid.

The Madrid Metro is a vital part of urban transportation in the city, facilitating the mobility of millions of passengers daily and providing essential connections for the entire region.

86

Carnivals in Spain are popular celebrations filled with music, parades, costumes, and color that embody the festive spirit before the start of Lent.

-Santa Cruz de Tenerife Carnival: It is one of the largest and most famous in the world, often compared to the Rio de Janeiro Carnival. Known for its impressive parades, carnival queens in elaborate costumes, and all-night parties.

-Cádiz Carnival: Famous for its "chirigotas," satirical music groups that present humorous and critical lyrics about society and politics. It also features parades, "comparsas," and an atmosphere full of music and joy.

-Águilas Carnival: Declared of International Tourist Interest, it is known for its spectacular parades with colorful costumes and floats. It includes the curious "Canto de la Mussona," an act symbolizing the struggle between the wild and the civilized.

-Badajoz Carnival: One of the most important in the Iberian Peninsula, it stands out for its parades with "comparsas" and "murgas," filling the streets with music and dancing.

-Sitges Carnival: Popular for its lively and carefree atmosphere and its Drag Queen Parade with colorful costumes. It is known for its LGBTQ+ friendly environment and the fun it offers.

-Las Palmas de Gran Canaria Carnival: It stands out for its Drag Queen Gala, an event that celebrates diversity, and its grand parade with "comparsas" and floats.

Each carnival has its own traditions and styles that reflect the cultural diversity of Spain, making them unique and popular events among locals and visitors alike.

87

The tallest buildings in Spain with their main features are:

1. Torre de Cristal (Madrid)
-**Height:** 249 meters.
-**Floors:** 52.
-**Function:** Offices and garden.
-**Construction year:** 2007-2009.
-**Interesting facts:** It was designed by César Pelli, an Argentine architect. It hosts a garden on the 49th floor, which is the highest in Spain.

2. Torre Cepsa (Madrid)
-**Height:** 248 meters.
-**Floors:** 45.
-**Function:** Offices.
-**Construction year:** 2004-2009.
-**Interesting facts:** Designed by Norman Foster, it was originally called Torre Repsol until it was acquired by the Cepsa Group.

3. Torre PwC (Madrid)
-**Height:** 236 meters.
-**Floors:** 52.
-**Function:** Hotel and offices.
-**Construction year:** 2004-2008.
-**Interesting facts:** Designed by Enrique Álvarez-Sala Walter and Carlos Rubio Carvajal, it hosts a luxury hotel, Eurostars Madrid Tower, on the first 31 floors.

4. Torre Emperador Castellana (Madrid)
-**Height:** 224 meters.
-**Floors:** 57.
-**Function:** Offices.
-**Construction year:** 1990-1993.
-**Interesting facts:** Originally known as Torre Espacio, it was one of the first buildings constructed in the Cuatro Torres Business Area.

5. Torre Intempo (Benidorm)
-**Height:** 202 meters.
-**Floors:** 47.
-**Function:** Residential.
-**Construction year:** 2007-2021.
-**Interesting facts:** The building consists of two towers connected by a central diamond-shaped core. Its construction took many years due to financial difficulties.

88

Andalusian horses, also known as Purebred Spanish Horses (PRE), are a horse breed originating from the Andalusia region in southern Spain.

They are known for their elegance, intelligence, and versatility, qualities that make them ideal for various equestrian disciplines, including classical riding.

1. History: They have a history dating back thousands of years. For centuries, they were bred by Carthusian monks and the nobility, particularly in the 15th and 16th centuries. They were used to improve other breeds, which has contributed to their worldwide reputation.

2. Physical Characteristics:
- **Height:** An average height of 1.55 to 1.65 meters.
- **Weight:** Between 450 and 550 kg.
- **Color:** Most commonly gray and bay, though black and chestnut horses are also found.
- **Conformation:** A compact body with a short back, well-developed hindquarters, and abundant mane and tail.
- **Temperament:** Known for their intelligence, gentle character, and willingness to learn. They are sensitive, which makes them receptive to human direction.

3. Uses:
- **Dressage:** They excel in this discipline due to their conformation and natural ability for piaffe and passage.
- **Doma Vaquera:** Used in the countryside for cattle handling.
- **Shows:** Often featured in equestrian exhibitions for their ability to perform exercises like the Spanish walk.
- **Carriages:** Also used in carriage events and competitions.

4. International Recognition: This breed has gained popularity outside of Spain for its impressive appearance and performance in competitions. They are considered ancestors of many modern breeds, such as the Lipizzaner, and have influenced the development of other European breeds.

5. Breeding and Conservation: Selective breeding is essential to maintain the desired characteristics. The National Association of Purebred Spanish Horse Breeders (ANCCE) is the entity in charge of registering this breed.

89

The longest rivers in Spain are among the most important in the Iberian Peninsula.

1. Ebro River:
-**Length:** Approximately 910 km.
-**Source:** Fontibre, Cantabria.
-**Mouth:** Ebro Delta, in the Mediterranean Sea.
-**Features:** The most voluminous river in Spain. It flows through varied landscapes, from mountains to plains.
-**Regions it flows through:** Cantabria, Castilla y León, La Rioja, Navarra, Aragón, and Catalonia.
-**Interesting facts:** It forms the largest delta in Spain and is vital for agriculture.

2. Tagus River:
-**Length:** Approximately 1,007 km.
-**Source:** Sierra de Albarracín, Teruel.
-**Mouth:** Atlantic Ocean, near Lisbon, Portugal.
-**Features:** The longest river in the Iberian Peninsula.
It flows through mountainous terrains and plains.
-**Regions it flows through:** Aragón, Castilla-La Mancha, Madrid, and Extremadura. In Portugal, it flows through regions until reaching Lisbon.
-**Interesting facts:** It hosts the Alcántara Reservoir, one of the largest in Europe.

3. Douro River:
-**Length:** Approximately 897 km.
-**Source:** Picos de Urbión, Soria.
-**Mouth:** Porto, in the Atlantic Ocean.
-**Features:** One of the main rivers for wine production in the Ribera del Duero region.
-**Regions it flows through:** Castilla y León, and it continues through Portugal.
-**Interesting facts:** It marks the natural border between Spain and Portugal in some stretches.

4. Guadalquivir River:
- **Length:** Approximately 657 km.
- **Source:** Sierra de Cazorla, Jaén.
- **Mouth:** Sanlúcar de Barrameda, in the Atlantic.
- **Features:** It is the only major navigable river in Spain.
- **Regions it flows through:** Andalusia (Jaén, Córdoba, Seville, and Cádiz).
- **Interesting facts:** It has been essential to the history of navigation and trade in Spain.

5. Guadiana River:
- **Length:** Approximately 744 km.
- **Source:** Near Ruidera, Castilla-La Mancha.
- **Mouth:** Border between Portugal and Spain, in the Atlantic.
- **Features:** It flows through a region rich in biodiversity, with significant wetlands.
- **Regions it flows through:** Castilla-La Mancha, Extremadura, and Andalusia, as well as Portugal.
- **Interesting facts:** It forms part of the border between Spain and Portugal in its middle section.

These rivers have been crucial to the history and development of the regions they flow through and continue to be important sources of water, energy, and transportation.

90

Spain has a rich musical tradition, and many of its musical instruments are emblematic of the country's cultural diversity.

1. Spanish Guitar (Classical or Flamenco Guitar):
-**Features:** Wooden body, nylon strings (classical) or metal strings (flamenco).
-**Sound:** Produces warm, resonant sounds.
-**Year of Creation:** The modern guitar was developed in the 19th century.
-**History:** It emerged from the vihuela and the baroque guitar. It is the main instrument in Spanish classical music and flamenco.

2. Castanets:
-**Features:** Small pieces of hard wood or fiber joined by a string.
-**Sound:** They produce a rhythmic clicking sound.
-**Year of Creation:** Although their origin is uncertain, they have been associated with Spain since the 16th century.
-**History:** Used in traditional music and flamenco, they are played between the fingers and the palm of the hand.

3. Bandurria:
-**Features:** A string instrument similar to the mandolin, with a tear-shaped soundbox.
-**Sound:** Produces bright, resonant sounds.
-**Year of Creation:** Its origin dates back to the 12th century, but the modern version appeared in the 19th century.
-**History:** Common in rondallas and folk music, especially in Castile.

4. Galician Bagpipe:
-**Features:** A wind instrument with bellows and blowpipes, similar to other bagpipes.
-**Sound:** Produces high-pitched, constant sounds.
-**Year of Creation:** Its origin is ancient, documented since the Middle Ages.
-**History:** Characteristic of Galicia, Asturias, and León, it is used in the traditional music of these regions.

5. Txalaparta:
- **Features:** A percussion instrument with wooden or stone boards placed on supports.
- **Sound:** Produces complex rhythms by striking the boards.
- **Year of Creation:** Traditionally used in the Basque Country for centuries.
- **History:** Originally used in rural festivities, it has now been revitalized in modern music.

6. Canary Timple:
- **Features:** A string instrument similar to the ukulele, with five strings.
- **Sound:** Produces high-pitched, bright tones.
- **Year of Creation:** Became popular in the 19th century.
- **History:** An emblem of the folk music of the Canary Islands.

7. Hurdy-Gurdy:
- **Features:** A string instrument with a rotating wheel, similar to a type of lute.
- **Sound:** Provides a constant buzzing and melodies.
- **Year of Creation:** Dates back to the Middle Ages.
- **History:** It was popular in medieval Europe and continues to be used in traditional Galician music.

91

The Tartessians, a legendary civilization of the Iberian Peninsula, captivate both archaeologists and literature enthusiasts.

They are believed to have flourished between the 12th and 6th centuries BCE, standing out as one of the region's oldest and most advanced cultures.

Their existence is shrouded in myths and legends, as the earliest references come from Greek and Roman texts, which mention Tartessos as a region rich in metals, with an advanced society and ruled by legendary monarchs such as Argantonio.

The economy of Tartessos revolved around metal trade, particularly copper and tin, trading with other Mediterranean cultures such as the Phoenicians.

Although little is known about their social and cultural structure, archaeological findings suggest a developed society with urban centers and refined art.

Discoveries at sites such as El Carambolo (Seville) and Cancho Roano (Badajoz) have provided clues about their lifestyle, though the remains found are fragmentary.

The exact location of Tartessos remains a mystery, though most theories place it in the south of the Iberian Peninsula, near the mouth of the Guadalquivir River, in present-day Andalusia.

However, no specific settlement has been definitively identified as Tartessos.

Moreover, the lack of direct written records complicates the historical verification of this civilization.

Despite the scarcity of concrete evidence, the legacy of Tartessos persists in Spain's historical memory, inspiring myths, literature, and speculation.

Its enigmatic history has been compared to Plato's Atlantis due to the descriptions of its wealth and prosperity.

Although mystery still surrounds its existence, the fascination with Tartessos remains alive, fueling the desire to unravel the secrets of this ancient civilization.

92

Silbo Gomero is a unique whistled language used on the island of La Gomera, in the Canary Islands.

It is known for its ability to allow communication over long distances, across the island's rugged mountainous landscape.

-History and Origins: Although its exact origin is unknown, it is believed to have been developed by the indigenous inhabitants, the Guanches, before the Spanish conquest. The first written records of Silbo Gomero date back to the 16th century. For centuries, the inhabitants of La Gomera used it to communicate in the island's rural areas.

-Linguistic Characteristics: Silbo Gomero is a substitute for spoken Spanish, converting words and phrases into whistles. It reproduces the vowels and consonants of Spanish using a series of tones and modulation. It uses two basic tones, high and low, to create different combinations that form words. Speakers can communicate any message in Spanish by transforming it into whistles, though decoding it requires skill.

-Function and Use: Originally, it was used to send messages across mountains and ravines, where direct oral communication was impossible due to distance and terrain. It could reach distances of up to 5 km, overcoming natural obstacles. Today, Silbo Gomero is more of a cultural curiosity than a necessary means of communication, but it remains a symbol of Gomera identity.

-Conservation and Recognition: In the late 20th century, Silbo Gomero was in danger of disappearing due to technological and social changes. However, the local government implemented educational programs to preserve it, even making its teaching mandatory in La Gomera schools. In 2009, UNESCO declared it an Intangible Cultural Heritage of Humanity, highlighting its cultural and linguistic significance.

-Present Day: Although it is no longer used as the primary means of communication, Silbo Gomero remains an essential component of La Gomera's cultural identity. It is taught to new generations to keep the knowledge of this ancient language alive and is performed at events and festivals for tourists and locals alike.

93

The Enchanted City is a unique natural site located near the town of Valdecabras, in the province of Cuenca.

It is known for its unique rock formations that resemble natural sculptures, shaped by erosion over millions of years.

-Geology and Formation: The rock formations of the Enchanted City originated during the Cretaceous period, approximately 90 million years ago. They are primarily composed of limestone, which was shaped by the action of water, wind, and climate changes.
Over time, erosion caused by these elements created whimsical figures that resemble sculptures, with shapes like bridges, animals, and mushrooms.

-Features and Route: The site covers about 250 hectares of rocky landscapes and forests. There is a marked circular trail of approximately 3 km that takes visitors through the most emblematic formations, such as the Roman Bridge, the Lovers of Teruel, the Face of the Man, and the Sea of Stone. The formations are named based on their resemblance to objects, animals, and human figures.

-History and Recognition: It was declared a Natural Site of National Interest in 1929, due to its geological uniqueness.
It is a popular tourist destination, offering a unique experience walking among the rocks sculpted by nature.
The Enchanted City has also been used as a setting in several films, such as "Conan the Barbarian" (1982) and "The World Is Not Enough" (1999).

-Mythology and Legends: As its name suggests, the Enchanted City is surrounded by myths and legends. It is said that the strange shapes of the rocks are the result of enchantments made by mythological beings.

94

Spain is known for its relaxed attitude towards naturism and boasts numerous nudist beaches, many of which are internationally recognized for their natural beauty and welcoming atmosphere.

1. Es Trenc (Mallorca):
- **Location**: On the southern coast of Mallorca, between the towns of Sa Ràpita and Colonia Sant Jordi.
- **Features**: Spanning over 3 km in length, this beach is famous for its white sand and turquoise waters, giving it a Caribbean-like appearance. It is divided into nudist and non-nudist zones, allowing everyone to enjoy the environment.
- **Services**: It offers basic amenities like beach bars and sunbed rentals, but maintains a natural atmosphere.

2. Playa de Ses Illetes (Formentera):
- **Location**: In the north of Formentera, within the Ses Salines Natural Park.
- **Features**: It is characterized by its crystal-clear waters and white sand. Although not entirely nudist, it is tolerant of naturism.
- **Recognition**: It is one of the highest-rated beaches in the world for its natural beauty.

3. Playa de Bolonia (Cádiz):
- **Location**: Near Tarifa, on the coast of Cádiz.
- **Features**: Known for its giant sand dune and clear waters. Nudism is common in the northern part, known as Playa de El Chorrito.
- **Attractions**: Besides the beach, you can visit the Roman ruins of Baelo Claudia.

4. Playa de Vera (Almería):
- **Location**: Near the town of Vera.
- **Features**: It is one of the few nudist beaches where there is also a nudist residential area and a naturist hotel.
- **Nudist Community**: The beach and its surroundings are known for their large nudist community that attracts visitors from all over the world.

5. Maspalomas Beach (Gran Canaria):
- **Location:** In the south of Gran Canaria.
- **Features:** This beach is famous for its sand dunes that resemble a desert. The central part is frequented by nudists.
- **Atmosphere:** It welcomes all types of visitors, from families to tourists who practice naturism.

6. Cavalleria Beach (Menorca):
- **Location:** In the north of Menorca.
- **Features:** A pristine beach with reddish sand surrounded by nature. Nudism is commonly practiced at the western end.
- **Access:** Requires a walk from the parking area, making it less crowded.

95
Christopher Columbus.

He is primarily known as the navigator who led the first documented European voyage to the American continent in 1492, an event that marked the beginning of the era of European exploration and colonization in the New World.

Over the centuries, there has been considerable debate about his exact birthplace, leading to various theories about his origin.

-Portuguese theory: There are theories suggesting that Columbus might have been born in Portugal.
These theories propose that he might have worked as a privateer for the Portuguese king before his expedition funded by Spain.

-Galician theory: Some authors argue that Columbus could have been Galician, based on documents suggesting family ties in Galicia.

-Catalan theory: Others suggest that Columbus might have been born in Catalonia, based on linguistic similarities in some of his writings and his connections with Catalan nobility.

-Genoese theory: It is said that Columbus was born in Genoa, in what is now Italy, in 1451. According to this version, his Italian name was Cristoforo Colombo. There are historical records and documents identifying him as a Genoese merchant.

96

Turrón is a traditional sweet that is especially consumed during the Christmas season in Spain.

-History and Origin: Turrón is believed to have its roots in the Arab world. It likely arrived on the Iberian Peninsula with the Arabs in the Middle Ages. The first written mention of turrón in Spain dates back to the 16th century and is associated with the city of Jijona (also known as Xixona), in Alicante.

-Ingredients and Varieties: The main ingredients of turrón are almonds and honey. Other components such as egg white and sugar can be added.

There are two main varieties of turrón:

1. Jijona turrón (soft): It has a soft and pasty texture. The almonds are finely ground, giving a consistency similar to a pâté.
2. Alicante turrón (hard): The almonds are kept whole and mixed with a syrup of honey and sugar, giving it a harder texture.
In addition to these classic varieties, there are many other versions, with chocolate, fruits, nuts, and other ingredients.

-Denomination of Origin: The Protected Designation of Origin (PDO) Jijona and Alicante Turrón guarantees the quality and origin of these products. Only nougats made in this region with the proper specifications can carry this label.

-Production and Tradition: The turrón-making process follows traditional methods. Almonds are roasted and then mixed with honey, sugar, and egg white. The mixture is slowly cooked until it reaches the desired consistency, then placed in molds to cool and solidify.

-Consumption: Although turrón is primarily associated with Christmas, it is available year-round. It is popular in many Spanish-speaking countries and is also consumed in Italy under the name "torrone."

-Curiosities: Turrón has been the focus of gastronomic competitions and festivals, such as the "Turrón Day" in Jijona.
The popularity of turrón has led to the creation of modern versions with innovative ingredients and unique flavors.

97

Spain has a rich tradition of alcoholic beverages that varies from region to region.

1. Cava:
-Information: A sparkling wine primarily produced in Catalonia, similar to champagne but made with different grape varieties.
-Origin: It emerged in the 19th century when Catalan producers adopted the traditional French method for making sparkling wine.
-Fun Facts: It is traditionally consumed during celebrations and festivities.

2. Cider:
-Information: A beverage fermented from apples, particularly popular in Asturias and the Basque Country.
-Origin: Cider has ancient roots in the Cantabrian region, with references dating back to the Middle Ages.
-Fun Facts: "Escanciado" is a special technique for serving cider, pouring it from a height to aerate it.

3. Vermouth:
-Information: A wine flavored with herbs and spices, typically consumed as an aperitif.
-Origin: Though originating in Italy, vermouth became popular in Spain during the 19th century.
-Fun Facts: The "hora del vermú" is a tradition where this drink is consumed before meals.

4. Sangria:
-Information: A drink made from red wine, fruit, and a touch of liquor, usually served with ice.
-Origin: Sangria is believed to have originated in the 18th century as a refreshing way to consume wine.
-Fun Facts: It is a popular drink among tourists and has become an international symbol of Spain.

5. Sherry:

-Information: A fortified wine originating from Jerez de la Frontera, in Andalusia. It is produced in a variety of styles, from dry to sweet.
-Origin: Sherry wine has a long history dating back to Roman times.
-Fun Facts: Shakespeare mentioned Sherry in several of his works, calling it "sack."

6. Orujo:
-Information: A high-proof spirit made in northern Spain from the solid residues of grapes.
-Origin: Its production is believed to have started in the Middle Ages, with monks making the liquor.
-Fun Facts: There is an annual Orujo festival in Potes, Cantabria, where traditional distillation techniques are showcased.

7. Anis:
-Information: A sweet liqueur flavored with anise, produced in various parts of Spain.
-Origin: Anise has been distilled in Spain since the 10th century, influenced by the Arabs.
-Fun Facts: Anís del Mono, produced in Badalona, is one of the most famous and features a distinctive bottle with a ribbed texture.

98

Chocolate with churros is a very popular traditional breakfast in Spain, especially in winter.

This dish consists of churros, which are fried dough shaped like sticks or spirals, and a thick hot chocolate.

-History: Although the exact origin of churros is uncertain, one theory holds that they were introduced to Spain by shepherds in the 16th century, who made a simple dough and fried it. Another theory suggests that they were brought by Portuguese traders after visiting China. Chocolate arrived in Spain from America in the 16th century, brought by the conquerors. It was initially consumed as a drink but was later thickened to be more like the chocolate we know today.

-Churros: Ingredients: They are made with a basic dough of flour, water, and salt. Some recipes also include oil or yeast.

-Churros Preparation: The dough is fried in hot oil in the form of long sticks or spirals. Traditionally, churreras, a type of pastry bag with a star-shaped nozzle, are used.

-Varieties: Churros can be thin and crispy, or thick and more fluffy, known as porras.

-Chocolate Ingredients: It is prepared with chocolate powder or bars, sugar, and milk or water.

-Chocolate Preparation: It is heated slowly, stirring until it reaches a thick consistency that allows for dipping the churros.

-Consumption: Chocolate with churros is usually consumed as breakfast or a snack, although it is also popular after a night out.
Churrerías, specialized places in churros, typically serve this dish freshly made.

-Custom and Tradition: It is usually consumed in winter, especially during holidays, but is also enjoyed throughout the year.
In Madrid, one of the most famous churrerías is Chocolatería San Ginés, which has been serving chocolate with churros since the 19th century.

-Fun Facts: There is a similar version in Mexico called "churros con chocolate," but the churros tend to be smaller and are sprinkled with sugar and cinnamon.

99

The Santa Compaña is a legend deeply rooted in the popular culture of Galicia, in the northwest of Spain.

It is described as a ghostly or spectral procession of tormented souls that wander through the forests and roads at night.

-Description and Features: The Santa Compaña is depicted as a nocturnal procession of spectral figures, generally dressed in white robes and carrying lit candles. The procession is usually led by a living person, who carries a cross and a cauldron of holy water. This living person is doomed to lead the procession until they find someone to replace them. Behind this leader, the tormented souls (often called "ánimas") walk in silence, and according to tradition, the procession can be detected by the smell of wax, the sound of distant bells, and the glow of the candles.

-Purpose and Meaning: The Santa Compaña is believed to visit homes where death is imminent, warning of the presence of a person who will soon pass away. The legend reflects popular beliefs about the afterlife and the fate of souls that have not found rest.

-Protection and Precautions: According to popular belief, there are certain measures one can take to avoid encountering the Santa Compaña:
1. Do not respond if one hears their name during the night.
2. Avoid crossing paths with the procession and make a cross on the ground.
3. If forced to lead the procession, avoid passing the cauldron or the cross to another person, as this condemns that person.

-Origin and Development: The exact origin of the Santa Compaña is uncertain, but it is related to ancient Celtic and Christian beliefs about death and ghosts. The legend has evolved over the centuries and varies in its details according to the region. There are similar variants in other parts of Spain and Europe, with different names and characteristics.

Cultural Impact: The Santa Compaña has inspired numerous works of literature, music, and art, exploring the mystery and fear associated with the legend. Even today, it remains alive in the collective memory of Galicia, and many claim to have seen or heard the Santa Compaña.

100

Spanish folklore is rich in fantastic creatures that reflect the history, mythology, and beliefs of the various regions of the country.

1. El Coco:
- **Origin:** Widespread in Spanish tradition and in Spanish-speaking countries.
- **Description and Characteristics:** A creature used to scare disobedient children. Representations vary from a shadow to a headless monster. It is believed to roam around houses at night to take away bad children.
- **Purpose:** It serves as an intimidating figure used to discipline children.

2. El Trasgu:
- **Origin:** Asturian folklore.
- **Description and Characteristics:** A mischievous elf, small and with a red hat. It has a hole in its right hand, which prevents it from carrying small objects.
- **Purpose:** It is a naughty being that causes disorder in homes at night.

3. La Sierpe:
- **Origin:** Various regions of Spain.
- **Description and Characteristics:** A giant snake or dragon, sometimes with magical features. It lives in lakes, mountains, and caves, and often guards treasures.
- **Purpose:** It can be a malevolent or benevolent figure, depending on the legend.

4. La Anjana:
- **Origin:** Cantabria.
- **Description and Characteristics:** Benevolent forest fairies, resembling beautiful women with wings. They dress in a radiant manner and often appear near springs and rivers.
- **Purpose:** They help travelers and those in need.

5. El Cuélebre:
- **Origin:** Asturias and Cantabria.
- **Description and Characteristics:** A winged snake or dragon. It dwells in caves and guards treasures and captive maidens.
- **Purpose:** It is attributed with great longevity, and its role is to protect treasures.

6. La Xana:
- **Origin:** Asturias.
- **Description and Characteristics:** A water nymph who lives in springs and rivers. She is beautiful and can grant treasures to those who pass her tests.
- **Purpose:** To protect bodies of water and grant treasures to the deserving.

7. El Basajaun:
- **Origin:** Basque Country and Navarra.
- **Description and Characteristics:** A hairy giant who lives in the forests and protects livestock. He has skills in teaching agricultural and craft techniques.
- **Purpose:** To protect the forest and teach techniques to humans.

8. La Güestia:
- **Origin:** Asturias.
- **Description and Characteristics:** Similar to the Santa Compaña, it is a procession of wandering souls that announces death.
- **Purpose:** To announce the death of those it visits.

9. Los Mouros:
- **Origin:** Galicia.
- **Description and Characteristics:** Magical beings who live underground and are associated with megalithic monuments. They are attributed with building these structures and guarding treasures.
- **Purpose:** To guard treasures and ancient structures.

101

Atlantis is an ancient myth described by the Greek philosopher Plato in his dialogues "Timaeus" and "Critias," which might be located in Spain.

According to Plato's description, Atlantis was an advanced and powerful civilization situated beyond the Pillars of Hercules (the Strait of Gibraltar) that was destroyed in a single day by a cataclysm.

Regarding the "Spanish Atlantis," the theory suggests that the lost civilization could be located on Spanish territory, based on research and local myths.

Some of the most **popular theories** include:

-**Doñana:** One possible location for Atlantis is mentioned as the Doñana National Park in Andalusia. In 2011, a National Geographic documentary suggested that the park's marshes might hide the remains of the lost civilization. This theory is based on satellite imagery and geological studies that show submerged structures, possibly attributed to the ancient civilization.
-**Tartessos:** Some scholars believe that Atlantis could have been confused with the civilization of Tartessos, located in the southwest of the Iberian peninsula, now Andalusia. Tartessos was an advanced civilization known for its wealth and trade; however, there is no definitive proof that Tartessos was Atlantis.
-**The Isle of Cadiz:** Another theory suggests that Atlantis could have been near the city of Cadiz, one of the oldest cities in Europe. Some research indicates that the underwater topography of the region could match Plato's descriptions.

Scientific Perspective:

Despite numerous theories and speculations, the existence of Atlantis has not been scientifically proven.
Most historians and archaeologists consider Plato's description to be a myth or political allegory.

Cultural Significance:

The idea of Atlantis has captured the imagination of many people for centuries. It has influenced literature, art, and popular culture, inspiring explorers, scientists, and writers.

Printed in Great Britain
by Amazon